T0196717

HEALING
THE
Soul

HEALING
THE
Soul
Releasing the
Effects of Trauma

TRISTAN FAITH, PHD

iUniverse

HEALING THE SOUL
RELEASING THE EFFECTS OF TRAUMA

iUniverse books may be ordered through booksellers or by contacting:

iUniverse
1663 Liberty Drive
Bloomington, IN 47403
www.iuniverse.com
1-800-Authors (1-800-288-4677)

ISBN: 978-1-5320-2346-0 (sc)
ISBN: 978-1-5320-2347-7 (e)

Library of Congress Control Number: 2017906884

Print information available on the last page.

iUniverse rev. date: 05/17/2017

The subject of regression therapy being used as a therapeutic process for healing trauma has been rejected and maligned by the traditional mainstream therapeutic community for decades. The recent work and books written by Dr. Brian Weiss have brought regression therapy, especially past life regression into the forefront as an alternative therapy. Dr. Weiss (1988) writes in his book "Many Lives, Many Masters": "The material tapped by past life therapy is in some ways like the powerful universal archetypes described by Carl Jung. However, the material of past life regression therapy is not archetypal or symbolic but actual memory fragments of the ongoing current of human experience from ancient times to the present".

The mind and body are a complex system of energetic thoughts and forms which are based on spiritual/scientific principals some of which being cause and effect. Often when we are experiencing tremendous emotional stress our bodies will mimic the emotions through physical illness, the same as when we are feeling exhilarated or happy our bodies experience more energy and vigor.

Leslie Takeuchi (2006) wrote in her report on "Cellular Memory in Organ Transplants":

"In my work with chronic pain populations, I have taken a closer look at this relationship of mind and matter, body and emotions, for keys to how people heal. In this search, I looked into theories of emotions or memories being somehow stored in the tissues of the body and later manifesting in the physical form of pain or disease. What was most striking were the numerous reports of organ transplant recipients who later experienced changes in personality traits, tastes for food, music, activities and even sexual preference."

Gary Schwartz, PhD and Linda Russek, PhD (1998) confirmed that concept when they wrote in their book "The Heart Code" that "all systems stored energy dynamically…and this information continued as a living, evolving system after the physical structure had deconstructed".

Ms. Takeuchi reported of a case of a seven-month old boy who received a heart transplant from a sixteen-month old boy who died from drowning. She stated that "the donor had a mild form of cerebral palsy mostly on the left side". As it turned out, the recipient developed the same form of palsy affect on his left side, although he had no prior symptoms before the transplant.

Clearly our cellular bodies remember their physical characteristics because they were designed for a specific purpose. Our bodies are like special order vehicles made to incorporate all that we have been, all that we are, and all that we will be. Our soul body uses the vehicle in order to enter into the world of matter so there is great relevance to the design of our form in helping us understand our soul's journey. Our body truly is a temple that houses the spiritual being.

If it is true that our organs carry their own story, could our emotions also have transferable memories? Leslie Takeuchi also told the story as reported by Dr. Paul Pearsall, who is a psychoneuroimmunologist. He recalled the story of an eight year old girl who received the heart transplant of a murdered ten year old girl. The heart recipient suffered from horrifying nightmares of the murder of her donor by a man she saw clearly in her dreams. The young girl was sent to see a psychiatrist where she gave graphic images and details of the murder and of the murderer. Her mother notified the police who found and easily convicted the murderer with the evidence provided by the frightened young girl. One can well imagine that the trauma suffered by the murdered young girl was registered within the cellular memories of her heart pounding in terror as she realized this strange man was about to murder her.

We also hear stories of amputees suffering what is called "phantom pain". The individual who has lost a body part will still feel as if they have the body part and that they are suffering pain in a region which does not exist, except in their mind. Sometimes I feel stabbing pain coming from an area of my abdomen where I had major surgery. There is actually nothing wrong with me, but the pain feels very real and present.

Often when individuals experience trauma they are unable to process the traumatic event and instead the mind compensates by repressing the memory until the person is strong enough or more capable of dealing with the traumatic information. Almost everything that happens to an individual has some relevance in their life, whether it shapes their belief system, how they perceive their environment and relationships, or how they view the very meaning of their life.

A repressed memory which expresses as an energetic imprint never goes away as it is stored in cellular memory as a dynamic force waiting for a trigger to rise to consciousness or until menacing thoughts surface in unconscious processes represented through our dreams, fears, nightmares, addictions, and patterns of dysfunctional behaviors that we often do not understand. I have often worked with people who suffer from night terrors and are afraid to be in the dark. Using regression therapy, we are able to trace their fears back to early childhood trauma. The individual now being able to bring their trauma to a conscious understanding becomes more empowered and able to comprehend the nature and events of their trauma giving them control over their fear. In the spiritual sense, one is bringing the darkness into the light.

My hypothesis is that all important information that has been accumulated by the journey of the individual's psyche or soul has been stored in cellular memories through an energetic orientation. These cellular memories include thoughts, feelings, beliefs perceptions, and images.

Dr. Candace Pert writes in her very informative book "Molecules of Emotion" Pert, 1997. p.141:

"The body is the unconscious mind! Repressed traumas caused by overwhelming emotion can be stored in a body part, thereafter affecting our ability to feel that part or even move it. The new work suggests there are almost infinite pathways for the conscience mind to access – and modify."

It is important to understand how our body and mind stores the energy of traumatic events as the information can help lead us to the ability to facilitate healing of psychological and physical trauma. Individuals who exist with a strong sense of victimization will be able to also find empowerment and psychological awareness as they understand part of the phenomena of the human journey also referred to as "The Hero's Journey". The very context of how one processes through trauma can be redirected by addressing the conscious and unconscious attributes of toxic sensory data as well as perceptions of objective reality. The redirection occurs when the traumatized individual is able to understand on a conscious level, the unconscious material which has a toxic affect due to the nature of its inability to integrate information with the conscious mind thereby enabling the completion of the "feedback loop" which will facilitate understanding and integration of the traumatic event.

Western science would have us believe that mental functions are linked to our brain's biological processes. Pharmacology would have us turn to medication as a way to alter or alleviate any discord in our mental or biological system. However, mind numbing drugs prove to be more of a quick fix Band-Aid used to cover a deep festering wound.

Traditional science holds to the belief that we evolved from a primeval chemical soup that organized itself partly by accident and part from natural selection into a complex multi-cellular organism with a central nervous system. This is a limited view of an infinitely complex system of energetic principles of consciousness which are in constant evolution in multiple dimensions.

Now quantum mechanics is recognizing a new field of "Quantum Wholeism" which attaches the idea that connection comes from interactive connections. The starting point for Quantum Wholeism is there is first a universal state and it breaks up into specifics. Past and futures are entangled to create wholes. If Newton was accurate when he said "what happens on one level, happens on all levels" much as the microcosm to the macrocosm, science will one day have to face the intrinsic complexities of life on the physical and mental plane as well as the astral. We are products of past, present and future actions as well as part of the collective conscious of our ancestors, societies, cultures and belief systems.

If all is consciousness which is an energetic principle, then awareness is the state of creation from consciousness. As we believe – we perceive and reality unfolds. Our biological form and mental function are a dynamic system of events which determine the unfolding of our lives for better or worse which is why we see some people are able to cure themselves from cancer and some are not. The determining factor is our belief systems and our ability to tap into the universal fullness of the cosmic energetic principle of active co-creation.

Stanislav Grof, M.D. (1990) wrote in his book "Holotropic Mind", "The exploration micro world soon revealed that the universe of everyday life which appears to us to be composed of solid, discrete objects, is actually a complex web of unified events and relationships".

Consciousness is active in its participation with the material world. Einstein taught us that space and time are integrated into a continuum known as "space time" which also means that we actually exist as one "continuous field of varying density". God said "Let there be Light" and then God created the "Word". First there was the thought or idea as the light was brought into the world and then the "word" or framing the idea started creation.

As a society we must be very aware and mindful of the thoughts that we use to interject into the fabric of the continuous field of consciousness as we hope to build a more homogenous world. Whether we know it or not, we are co-creating players in this continually evolving world of wonders. Wherever we place our attention, there we are. If we believe in the beauty and goodness of the world, we will create it so. However, it is not quite such a simple solution to think good thoughts as what we believe, think and feel must be congruent.

We can place our thoughts on the desire to obtain money, a good relationship, or even happiness, however if we believe we "don't deserve these things" or that "things just don't work out for us" in our deepest thoughts we are giving mixed messages to our body and mind. The incongruence of negative thoughts cancels out our positive desires. In many cases the negative beliefs actually draw us into negative experiences as "like energy attracts like energy".

Many people voice positive thoughts while in their hearts they wait for something negative to happen. Sometimes they live in a quiet fear of what they do not want coming into their lives, which actually draws the fear to them. They are dramatically affected by events that are outside their control and yet take the issues personally fueling a belief that they are doomed or even worse, that God has forsaken them.

One must be strong, courageous and relentless in their conviction about creating the life they want. One must also think about Karma and the highest good because if we use a narcissistic approach to securing our desires, there will also be retribution. This is not to say if you want a Porsche and you work hard to purchase it, that there is anything wrong with getting the car of your dreams. However, if the money came to purchase the car because you cheated another person out of money, your desire would now become your problem as there is always a price to pay for wrongful acts. With consciousness, desires have less power and you might feel just as good driving a gas efficient Prius, but that is another story.

Benjamin Franklin understanding the illusiveness of our critical awareness, stated in "Poor Richards Almanac"; *"There are three things extremely hard: steel, a diamond, and to know one's self."* Trauma, prejudice, unfounded beliefs, negative thoughts, misleading desires, and self-destructive behaviors interfere with our ability to know the very essence of our being. Regression therapy can assist in the process of uncovering our karmic connection to psyche and to the universal mind. Regression therapy can also help heal the trauma by transmuting the negative cellular memory stored in the body as well as bringing to consciousness those feelings that have held us captive to negative patterns. Through releasing the negative energy otherwise noted as cellular imprint, integrating the newly realized unconscious material from the regression and bringing new awareness and feelings of empowerment into the mental awareness of the individual subject, one is finally able to successfully complete the feedback loop in a positive way. The person moves from a state of unconscious reaction to a more desired state of pro-action as well as feelings of being more in control of their life.

When we are able to integrate the aspects of the unconscious with the conscious, we are more likely to become empowered and relieved of our anxiety as well as the effects of trauma producing symptoms. Instead of being caught in our own individual stories, we can move into the roles of actor and director in our wonderful adventure of life. Somehow we are all linked together in this world as an expression of this world as well as a creative aspect of the cosmic consciousness.

The lesson of "Seek ye within" and "Know thyself" demonstrates to us that the answers that we need as well as the healing we desire are held within the deep recesses of our mind and soul. Traditional science might take issue with the ominous lack of biological clarity; however, medicine and psychology are still in infant stages when addressing the issues of the unconscious and the energetic system of the body.

In 2005 I met a powerful and influential lawyer at an art opening in Santa Fe who had just broken his arm in a skiing accident. He was on the board for a scientific think tank which was biologically focused. I explained to him the importance of the unified force field or "God factor" and told him I could prove it by healing his broken arm. The price I would charge was to have energy work included in the scientific research.

I spent over a half hour working as a conduit sending light and energy into the affected area of his arm along with my prayers for healing. I informed him that his arm would feel much better by tomorrow, but he would still have minor pain for a short time.

The next day the man reported that his arm was feeling much better and a week later when he returned to his physician in California for X-rays there was no sign of a break.

I received an email from the man stating: "Interestingly, my orthopedic surgeon in LA took four X-ray images when I saw him on Wednesday this week. None showed the crack in the humerous which appears clearly in one of the two x-rays taken in Taos. My doctor thinks that his pictures were taken at the wrong angle. I wonder if the absence of a crack might have something to do with you."

Actually the healing had little to do with me and much more to do with the cosmic creator principle working through me. That same force also worked through me when I healed other broken bones, cancers, and a case of hydrocephalus. These could be counted as miraculous healings which seems contrary to the medical model. Somehow I am able to become a catalyst to physical attunement through supra-conscious forces. Matthew 19:26 tells us that Jesus said "through god all things are possible".

I have witnessed a rose bush in my yard in January sitting amidst ice and snow burst into full bloom being covered by red roses in the dead of winter. I watched orbs of light floating in a room as I was having tea with a friend. I have talked to the dead and floated bewildered above my body. I have worn the mark of stigmata and been kissed by a Hindu saint. Since being a child of twelve, I have seen UFO's of various constructs and meditated in a crop circle in England as a crop circle formed next to me in a matter of a few minutes. I have met many people who have similar experiences, in part due to their willingness to partake of life's currently unexplainable mysteries.

St. Ansel of Canterbury (1100) stated, "I do not seek to understand that I may believe, but I believe in order to understand". Perhaps it is the belief and openness to mystical experience that opens the door to possibilities.

I have no scientific proof and yet in each case I know that it is the medical model that is the fumbling child in the room and it is spirit that waits patiently for the adulthood to emerge. I cannot label these events as I know too little to address the universal constructs, but I do know that we are much more than we imagine. To reach for consciousness is to invite the mysteries to unfold. To live in an ego based desire to create the world as we would have it offers only limited supply of the physical manifestation.

What Is Trauma

I am the product of my environment, my socialization, my heritage and most of all, my own thoughts. We have evolved, but not as a substance which haphazardly crawled from the primordial soup, instead, as an energetic expression of the cosmic consciousness which maneuvers through a universal law of cause and effect.

The cosmos, the world of matter, and humanity exists as consciousness desired a way to experience the creative aspects of consciousness through awareness. We are born of the paradox, the ouroboros, and the ying/yang of existence spurred on by diametrically opposing forces pushing against the center, churning, dancing, colliding in search of equilibrium, and in search of self-revelation.

We search for happiness believing it to be an absolute right. We even put it in our Constitution. We search for love believing it an ultimate goal. We build fantasies in our minds about what happiness will look like and sometimes we find the reality of our dreams.

Happiness is subjective and often illusive in its subjectivity. Part of our human dynamic is the built in predisposition to the desire for happiness. Trauma occurs as a challenge to our perceptions about what we expect life to look like. Do the Gods throw us curveballs to test our strength, our will, or our courage, or does trauma emerge out of our own karmic dispensation?

In the depths of trauma, we cry out to God, we curse God, and we wonder why we have been abandoned. Our search for meaning has little value as trauma brings us face to face with what seems unconscionable. The very foundation of our inherent inclination toward happiness is shattered in the face of trauma. The victim is catapulted into an abyss of confusion as their senses are overwhelmed by a new sense of being in the world. Life becomes unsafe and trauma thrusts one flailing into the dark sea of the unknown, incalculable existence. Survival becomes the goal as the senses of the migdula move into fight, flight or freeze.

I had a teacher who said; "What we resist, persists". Another teacher taught: "What we most fear is what we will draw to us". I have found both statements to be true. Unresolved trauma develops its own life as it creeps into our unconscious like screams in our dreams. Glimpses of distorted images poking through the fog, moments of terror, internal voices provoking fear, insecurity and distrust are the residues made from trauma.

The predatory individual can sniff out the fear and instability in a traumatized person as if they emit some strange pheromone driven signal that says "come and get me as I am wounded and helpless". For some unlucky individuals, trauma becomes a way of life as they are drawn to one predator after another laying out a passageway for abuse. Sometimes a traumatized individual just believes that this is their lot in life and so when the maladaptive behavior occurs long enough, eventually the idea of happiness is a far too distant fading vision and trauma is their everyday friend.

So common is the adaptive behavior of traumatized individuals that psychologist have given it a name. The "Stockholm Syndrome" is the term given to describe the emotional bonding of a traumatized individual to their abuser. The victim begins to see themselves as flawed rather than view the abuser as the problem.

The Stockholm Syndrome

The condition was first noticed when machine gun toting bank robbers entered a bank in Stockholm, Sweden, guns blasting and held four terrified hostages for the next 131 hours. The bank robbers strapped dynamite to the hostages and held them in a bank vault until their rescue by the police.

The hostages that had been abused, threatened, and in fear of losing their lives for five days, shocked the public by exhibiting emotional "bonding" with their captors. The hostages even believed that the criminals were protecting them from the police. One woman hostage became engaged to one of the criminals while another hostage set up a legal defense fund to help the bank robbers with legal fees.

One of the components necessary for the "Stockholm Syndrome" to occur is time. Research has shown that in hostage situations that occur over a short span of time, individuals have not been exposed to the abuse long enough to develop fantasies as coping strategies.

I watched an interview on 20/20 with a fourteen-year-old girl who had been abducted by a person she knew and trusted. He held her captive for several months mentally and physically abusing her as well as repeatedly raping her. The reoccurring trauma actually changed the girl's personal identity as well as her perceptions of reality. The abuser moved the girl from hotel to hotel; home schooled her and gave her a different name.

Police were called by a suspicious hotel worker and as they came to rescue the young girl she did not view the police as rescuers, but as dangerous intruders. When the police asked her repeatedly what her name was, the girl answered with the false name given to her by her kidnapper.

In the face of hopelessness, the young girl had given up her previous identity in an effort to survive her ordeal. She surrendered to her new circumstance and in an effort to find some positive aspect of her predicament she began to believe and collaborate with her abductor. In him, she looked for threads of humanity to sustain her own need for love or belonging. Other situations which fall under the perimeters of the "Stockholm Syndrome" would be individuals who suffered from; child abuse, battered/abused women, prisoners of war, cult members, incest victims, criminal hostage situations, concentration camp prisoners, and people in controlling or intimidating relationships.

I would venture to guess that many individuals at one point in their lives have found themselves in a trauma producing episode whether it was being raised in a highly dysfunctional family, participating in high risk situation such as war, being physically, mentally, or sexually abused over a period of time, being involved in high risk activity such as gang involvement especially where there is criminal activity, and simply working for a heartless controlling boss or corporation that keeps you in continual fear pertaining to your financial security.

As a therapist in a treatment center, I worked with a ten-year-old boy who always had a big smile accented by his baby round cheeks. He was born to a teenage mother, fatherless except for the sperm donor who helped give him life, and he lived in a gang infested environment. His mother was hard working, loving, and did the best she could to raise her son, but she could not protect him from the dark reality of the streets.

The boy was suffering from trauma because he woke up one morning in bed as a young child to find his aunt lying next to him dead from a drug overdose. The trauma continued as the gangs pressured him to join and he lived in daily fear of the day that his life would also end because of drugs or gang revenge. In certain areas of our country it is not safe to be a young boy on your own, especially if you have a gentle nature. No matter how dangerous gang membership might be it is still safer than the alternative of living on your own without membership protection.

The young boy relayed the story to me about how he had been picked up in a car at age ten by some of the older gang members. The boys drove around for a while and then handed him a hand gun, drove to a specific area, pointed out a young man and told him to shoot. The young boy faced a dilemma as he did not want to kill anyone, but to be seen as a coward would have severe consequences. My client reported pulling the trigger, but luckily missing the target. This incident is not an uncommon event in gang life.

While living in Chicago I attended a holocaust benefit with a Jewish friend of mine. I listened intently as an ex-Nazi soldier talked about growing up in Germany as part of Hitler's Youth Movement which had mandated attendance required by Adolf Hitler for all young German children. He relayed the story about how the young boys were given puppies to take home and care for. After months of bonding, feeding, playing with and loving their new wards, the boys were told to bring their puppies to the next meeting. They were then made to kill their puppies with their bare hands.

Hitler actually used trauma as a way to emotionally shut down these boys by having them strangle their dogs and imprint an illogical obedience in their psyche. In many ways, gangs have developed the same methodology when they force younger members to do acts of violence out of fear of rejection and or physical repercussions.

One of the strategies individuals use for survival during times of trauma come from the old adage "if you can't beat them, join them".

If one feels they have no control in the situation or they are afraid of rocking the boat and making matters worse, it appears easier or safer for them to resign to the situation and reframe their belief system to that of the abuser.

That is why women who have been beaten by their husbands say "they deserved it" or children that are being sexually abused by parents withhold the information. I had worked with many abused children who thought they had done something wrong. On some level they have bought into the sickness caused by their victimizer that tells them they do not deserve love, kindness and respect. The greatest fear most people have is the fear that they are unlovable and some people will suffer and endure the greatest abuses hoping somehow the abuser will change their ways and love them. Many people also have a great desire to be accepted and belong to a family, group, or a social status.

There is also the fear of change. What will happen to me if I don't tolerate the abuse? Where will I go and how will I survive. I have found that many of the children and teens that I have worked with as a therapist are living life in survival mode which means they live in constant fear of what each day brings with no hope for the future and they trust no one. Life does not offer them an exciting adventure, but rather a world filled with traps and unpredictable mishaps. Some individuals live in an environment where there is ever present in their minds the threat of real and perceived dangers.

While working as a day treatment therapist I worked with a bright and creative thirteen-year-old boy whose foster parents were heroin addicts. The father had actually served jail time for beating the mom so badly she had to be hospitalized. The boy regularly reported being physically abused by the foster parents. During the family meetings, the parents were surprisingly abusive to me, often screaming and slamming doors. They talked to the boy in shaming ways and criticized his every move. I could not help but wonder if this was how they acted in front of the therapist, how was their behavior towards the boy at home behind closed doors.

I regularly reported the foster parents to child protective services and wrote referrals for the boy to be put with another family. Child protective services eventually told me to stop calling and threatened my credentials. When CPS would show up at the home, the parents knew exactly the right act to put on for the social worker. The foster parents would also report how horrible the boy was and how I had been fooled by him. The truth was that the boy was highly intelligent, earned good grades and had an exceptional gift for writing, but due to the desperation of his situation he was becoming more and more maladaptive, manipulative, and hopeless.

A major shift occurred after he ran away from home one night after being abused. He traveled several miles through the night and was found by staff sleeping on the stoop outside of my office door. Taking a tremendous leap of courage, the boy had decided to try to make a break. He begged to be placed anywhere away from his home including residential treatment which was run much like prison, but I was unable to help him. I called every agency I knew as well as several calls to my supervisor trying to arrange at least temporary placement, but there was no help. Eventually, they boy became so maladaptive and rebellious; I was able to talk the foster parents into letting him go to residential treatment. Psychologists would say that the boy's "Cognitive Dissonance" had finally given away.

Cognitive Dissonance

L eon Festinger first coined the term "Cognitive Dissonance" in 1956 after he observed members of a cult who were willing to give up their homes, jobs, and nuclear families in order to participate in a shared belief. The members firmly believed that end times were coming and that they would be saved by flying saucers before a great flood hit the earth.

Obviously, the flood did not happen and the spaceships did not take anyone away, but the members had to believe their scenario strongly enough to change everything they previously believed about their lives. "The moral"; hypothesized by Leon Festinger[1](1962) "the more you invest (income, job, home, time, effort, etc.) the stronger your need to justify your position. If you invest everything you have, it requires an almost unreasoning belief and unusual attitude to support and justify that investment". This is the stuff fanaticism is made of.

We have seen a repeat of this scenario with the mass suicide of over 900 people living with cult leader Jim Jones in Guyana, South America.[2] The deaths were linked to the killing of five people on a fact finding mission sent by the United States government on behalf

---

[1]   Festinger, L. Theory of Cognitive Dissonance. 1962, Stanford, California, Stanford University Press.

[2]   Nightmare in Jonestown. Time Magazine. December 1978 1204

of concerned relatives. Among the five killed by Jones followers was a U.S. Congressman Leo Ryan. Jim Jones then ordered the members of his cult which consisted of men, women and children to drink cool aid laced with cyanide.

On March 26, 1997 police discovered thirty-nine members of the Heaven's Gate cult who had committed suicide. Marshall Applewhite (1997) the leader had indoctrinated them into the belief that a UFO would take their souls to another "level of existence above human".

There are several types of investments that keep us from discovering or uncovering the roots of trauma. One is the "emotional investment" which can allow individuals to accept harmful dysfunctional relationships due to the amount of emotional effort and time spent with their spouse, partner, family member, or friend. We do not want to accept the reality of the wasted effort. Another type of investment is "social investment" which is the desire to avoid social embarrassment or ostracizing. Many couples are concerned about the "family investment" which guides decisions based on the perceived needs of the children and for many people the "financial investment" holds the victim in the relationship as the controlling or abusive partner often controls the financial aspects of material survival. Many people in today's work place are feeling a level of trauma and cognitive dissonance as they are required to work longer hours, earn less money and act in uncaring ways as required by their company or work place.

Cognitive dissonance would be a contributing factor for scientists and researchers rejecting the concept of reincarnation. How would the world change if we actually knew we would have to "reap what we sow" or that the environment we are destroying will actually be the place that we will return to in the future?

What would life be like if people no longer took advantage of others knowing that they were only hurting themselves in the end. The relevance of understanding Karma is to know that we are all part of an interconnected woven fabric and that its strength is determined from the integrity of the fibers. I imagine the world consciousness currently as looking a bit like grandmother's patchwork quilt hidden in a dank closet that has areas of fabric eaten by moths, fibers dingy and torn from neglect with occasional patches of beautiful fabric with lovingly placed stitches.

Fear, greed, selfishness, apathy, trauma, ignorance, arrogance and ethnocentricity are prevalent and deteriorating factors that eat away at the fabric of our interconnectedness. We can look to places like Findhorn, Scotland, which is a community that flourished in the 1960's by recognizing the interconnectedness of all creation.

The Findhorn community was known for their incredible ability to tap into the unseen energies of nature as well as make a conscious relationship working with the energies to create a beacon for humanity becoming pioneers in gardening, living in spiritual community and having a conscious relationship with nature. The amazing flowers and vegetables grown at Findhorn are internationally renowned for their size, taste, smell and superior plant quality.

David Spangler (2012) stated in an article on the Findhorn website: "What made the community was the fact that individuals had their own private practice of attuning to their inner divinity, each person in his or her own unique way, and then sharing the fruits of that not necessarily in the form of guidance, but in the form of love and compassion, fellowship and goodwill and a loving energy throughout the day." Findhorn can certainly be seen as an antidote and alternative to many of our current trauma producing lifestyles where there is social unrest and economic suffering.

Collective Trauma

A good example of trauma experienced on a social or national level is the events that occurred on and after 9/11. Many people have been traumatized by the horrendous collisions of the planes that were flown into the Twin Towers in New York City by terrorists. Whether they were onlookers trapped in this nightmare or viewed the carnage in the comfort of their homes watching TV, everyone I spoke to, experienced the traumatic effects of the event.

Dr. Hongtu Chen (2003) and his associates organized a study which surveyed 555 residents from a neighborhood close to the world trade center to examine the psychological impact from the 9/11 disaster. The results state: [3]

> "Prevalent anxiety was found in general among community residents and additional depression in those who lost family members or friends. The mental health condition of the community improved tremendously five months later with the initial 59% of general residents having 4 or more emotional

---

[3]   Chen, Hongtu. Dr. Emotional Distress in a Community At The Terrorist Attact On The World Trade Center. Community Mental Health Journal, Vol.39, No. 2, April 2003

symptoms dropping to 17%. However more than half
of the community residents had persistently shown
one or more symptoms of emotional distress."

According to the "Stockholm Syndrome" a single event would not
have perpetuated enough trauma for individuals to change their belief
systems. Interestingly, for weeks following the 9/11 attack people were
continually barraged with media coverage of the disaster, stories about
the families who lost loved ones and the horror of the heroic firemen
who lost their lives trying to save others. Most importantly were the
continued reports of terrorist threats as anthrax was reported to be
found in various places throughout the United States. People were
told there was a threat of chemical warfare being used in their towns
and police and military presence visually insured heightened anxiety
levels in the general population. A perfect scenario was carried out on a
large national basis to insure the "Stockholm Syndrome" was effective
throughout the United States.

Many people became fearful, isolated themselves, wanted revenge,
wanted assurance of their safety, wanted their lifestyle protected, and
were willing to give up hard earned constitutional rights in order that
they might feel safer. The United States became a police state with the
help of "The Patriot Act".

Terrorism became a threat to many individual's perceived notions
about their safety and so on a mass level, Americans complied with
government demands to give President Bush full authority to eliminate
Habitués Corpus, Miranda Rights, and to allow search and seizure
without a warrant. Few people actually read the Patriot Act or cared
about the contents as they were now in coercion with the abuser and
willing to relegate personal responsibility and personal discernment.

When President Bush told the American public that we needed to
go into Iraq because Sadam Hussain had weapons of mass destruction,

people rallied to war even though there was no real evidence to the claim. As far as retaliation for 9/11, Bin Loden had already shown up on our TV's taking the credit for the destruction and he was a Saudi Arabian Citizen who was probably living somewhere in Afghanistan or Pakistan. The collapse of the three towers still prompts unanswered questions as only two towers were hit by planes. The anthrax scares were never traced to anyone and seemed to disappear into oblivion.

Many people became disassociated from the truth in order to adopt a belief system built from their perception of a desire to survive in a hostile environment. Cognitive dissonance occurs when there is an unreasoning belief that supports, bonds and justifies our position to act in unhealthy and destructive ways, be it to ourselves or others. There are few people who have not felt the effects of the victimization of trauma. There are many people who cannot express or acknowledge the devastating effects that trauma has caused in their lives.

Within the United States another kind of trauma was unfolding after 9/11. Jennifer Bryan at Yale University discussed the cultural trauma experienced by the Muslim community in Jersey City after 9/11. Many of the Muslims she interviewed were actually from Egypt, Tunisia, and Morocco. The Muslims reported raids on their homes and businesses; the FBI and Homeland Security arrested and questioned hundreds of Arabs from their Jersey City homes. Many employers were reluctant to hire Muslims and landlords imposed large increases in the rents that were being charged to Muslim tenants.

Bryan (2004) reported:[4] "A puzzling coalition of non-Muslims from diverse ethnic groups including Italian Americans and African Americans who had shared a long history of intergroup conflict in Jersey City, formed an unprecedented alliance to "watch" Arab Muslims for

---

[4]   Bryon, J. L. "In Search of the True Islam: The Impact of 9/11 On Muslims in Jersey City". 2004 8-14

suspicious activities". In addition, the alliance used telescopes to spy on the Muslims in their homes, organized patrols near schools and mosques as well as physically and verbally assaulted, harassed and intimidated Muslims.

Muslim women took the main brunt of the abuse from non-Muslims as they reported being punched in the face, beaten, clothes ripped off and veils torn. Muslim children reported being beaten up and bullied in schools. In Part, the abusive behaviors by citizens against Muslims was prompted by President Bush's claim of "sleeper cells" living in communities just waiting to be activated into terrorism.

While the Muslim community lived in fear and trauma under constant threat from their abusers, they also adapted the "Stockholm Syndrome" posture. Their response was to become shining examples of "The True Islam" in an effort to win favor with their abusers. The Muslim men gathered with a Sheik or Imam to study the Quran and many more relaxed Muslims went back to their traditional practices moving away from American vices such as drinking, smoking, and going to night clubs. Rather than fighting their abusers which surely would have brought great harm to the Muslim community, they decided to build positive feelings among non-Muslims by becoming model citizens and a unified spiritual community.

"The True Islam" resurgence within the Muslim community rekindled a collective identity. The Muslims of Jersey City gained a renewed sense of purpose and empowerment through their religion. While trauma and fear are still part of their experience and perceptions, purpose gives resilience, courage and perseverance.

On some levels the trauma suffered by the Muslim community at the hands of non-Muslim Americans reminds me of the moral dilemmas in the movie "The Dark Knight" in which good and righteous men through a series of traumatic events turn to the dark side. In the movie there is a District Attorney, Harvey Dent who is a moral and caring man that after being grotesquely disfigured by Batman's arch nemesis "The Joker", becomes hateful, seeking vengeance on all the people he considers culpable for his tragedy. Even Batman, in his determination to catch the "Joker" begins to ignore his moral code and justify injustice.

Repeated trauma blurs their perception of what is right and what is wrong, especially if they are operating in a perceived survival mode. We are all capable on some level of crossing boundaries, moving from light to dark, justifying the unjust depending on the point where trauma leads us to the breaking point of losing our ability to care about ourselves and others. After enough assaults to our emotional and intellectual being, the mind will go into overload and survival is the only motivation and life goal.

Historical Trauma

B efore leaving to attend classes in England, I attended a conference in Albuquerque, New Mexico in July of 2008. The topic was "historical trauma" especially related to the Native American population as the gathering was sponsored by the New Mexico Native American Cultural Center.

There is currently a movement within the Native American community to add "Historical Trauma" as a diagnosis listed in the DSMIV, which is a diagnostic tool for therapists and psychiatrists which defines the criteria for mental illness and its diagnosis. The idea of historical trauma as a diagnosis is based on the fact that many of the Native American population share common effects and symptoms from trauma related to their history of European aggression and genocide in addition to being treated as second class citizens. Based on a commonly shared history of trauma, abuse, dehumanization perpetuated by another cultural group and collective genocide brought upon the Native population by European groups we see a common collective pattern of mental health issues, especially depression and addiction. A similar diagnosis could also be used by forced relocation and abuse of people of African descent, holocaust victims, the Irish and Chinese immigrants or any other group that suffered severe and long standing trauma at the hands of another collective cultural group.

According to David Stannard in his book American Holocaust; he estimates the holocaust of Native populations in North America to be "100 million for the hemisphere and 18 million for the people north of Mexico. In 1910 the total population of Native Americans was about 400,000, down from 18 – 19 million in 1492." The Native American holocaust is probably one of the largest mass exterminations the world has ever known.

As I looked around the large conference room choking back my own tears at such a revelation, I saw evidenced through the deep sadness in the faces of the mostly Native American attendees, the painful impact still stinging into their psyches from their own historical trauma. What must it feel like to know there was a race of humans that wanted your complete annihilation and did their best to make it happen. Many of the Native participants at the conference seemed to still be held captive by their historical trauma and were suffering on some level from "Stockholm Syndrome" and "cognitive dissonance" as they were locked into unfounded belief systems often originated and amplified by their aggressors. Many still suffered lives of family abuse, addiction, and negative patterns of behavior.

Often the most diabolical perpetrator is the victim's own perception about their inability to escape their predicament. If one is able to understand the fallacy of a flawed ideology as well as calculate the motivation, symptoms of trauma would be greatly reduced and the individual could move more easily into feelings of empowerment.

Indigenous culture's belief systems include personal and community attunement with the energetic principle of the natural world as well as the creator spirit which exists in all things. Native culture that believes in "Historical Trauma" also believes in the energetic or cellular lineage and continued existence of the ancestors in spiritual form who still remain linked to their descendants. Time and space dimension does not hold the same meaning for indigenous cultures as for the European Western culture and they are often more attuned to natural phenomena.

When I went to participate in a sweat lodge with a Native American medicine man during a serious illness hoping the sweat would help me, the medicine man pulled me aside. He did not want me to do the sweat due to my illness, but offered to do a healing ceremony for me. The medicine man floated through time and space mystically moving the energy and calling on the healing powers. I felt better immediately. After a good night sleep, I awoke to find myself almost recovered, although the illness had been lingering for over two weeks.

The traumatizing effects felt by some of the Native American people due to the abuse brought to them by the Europeans has in some cases paralyzed their ability to perceive ways to develop a happy healthy life based on their own chosen cultural and social values. Fortunately, much is changing now in the culture, partly due to the economic impact brought by the Casinos which gives them the financial freedom to choose their own path. Another problem is the neuro-pathways of the brain develop synapses or electrical charges that continue to stimulate the feelings related to trauma causing circular thought patterns which often evoke feelings of anger and despair as individuals are left unable to complete the feedback loop and process through the negative impact of trauma. Often when a victimized individual develops the capability to shift their perspective and perception about the causes and effects of their situation as well as develop a sense of empowerment, there is a possibility of transmuting the negative effects of trauma into a character strengthening orientation which develops courage, compassion, and self-determination.

Symptoms and Effects of Trauma

The effects of traumatic experiences occur when individuals find themselves confronted suddenly by some kind of unexpected danger that delivers a severe threat to their existence as they perceive it to be. Common traumatic experiences include physical or sexual attack, a serious illness, serious accident, victim of natural disaster such as fire, flood, hurricane, or tornado, animal attack, witness or victim of a shooting, victim or witness to domestic violence severe bullying or ridicule.

Individuals who experience traumatic events have varying degrees of symptoms based on the person's own natural ability to cope and assimilate the emotions of the traumatic event. Personal resiliency is also a factor. Additionally, support from family, friends, and professionals can help lighten the burden of stressors incurred by the traumatic event.

Often people affected by trauma have trouble understanding what has happened to them as they can repress some of the memories related to the trauma. Also some people think they did something wrong that contributed to the events, or other individuals lose their grip on reality as their life has been changed dramatically.

Once a person has experienced the terrorizing fear of being totally helpless, especially when there is senseless violence added to the trauma, their perception of the world is greatly changed as they no longer view the world as a safe place to be. Some survivors turn to drugs and alcohol as a way to block the overwhelming feelings of fear and helplessness.

Other symptoms developed due to the effects of trauma are flashbacks, nightmares, repeating upsetting memories, getting upset when triggered by a trauma related sight, sound, smell, feeling or taste, anxiety,

Now that I have addressed the roots of trauma as well as the symptoms and results of trauma, it is important to understand how the aspects of reincarnation and karma can have an effect on the individual's response to trauma.

The very nature of response to trauma is to build psychological resistance to the incident. Sigmund Freud (1911) presented a paper "Remembering, Repeating, and Working Through"[5] where he addressed the treatment of trauma using psychoanalysis. "In its first phase that of Breuer's catharsis – it consisted in bringing directly into focus the moment at which the symptom was formed, and in persistently endeavoring to reproduce the mental processes involved in that situation, in order to direct their discharge along the path of conscious activity."

After being traumatized an individual will build a resistance to remembering what happened. Freud continues to explain that what a person has forgotten or repressed due to trauma "he reproduces not as a memory but as an action: he repeats it, without, of course, knowing that he is repeating it". The unconscious mind must bring to light that which has been suppressed so that it can consciously comprehend its dilemma and bring conscious mind and subconscious mind to congruency. I read somewhere that Freud once said something to the effect when the conscious mind and subconscious mind do battle; the subconscious mind will ultimately always win.

---

[5] Strachey, James. Sigmund Freud, 1911, London, England: The Hogarth Press.

Reincarnation

Socrates stated "I am confident that there truly is such a thing as living again, that the living spring from the dead, and the souls of the dead are in existence."

Many people have questioned me about my ideas of reincarnation, asking if we do not just make up the stories. Admittedly, I had the same question when I first started facilitating past life regressions, however most of the stories were about simplistic miserable lives and there was much emotion involved in the telling.

Dr. Edith Fiore makes a case for reincarnation as she states in her book "You Have Been Here Before". "Are they putting on an act? If so most should be nominated for Academy Awards. I have listened for thousands of hours. I am convinced there is no deliberate attempt to deceive. The tears, shaking, flinching, smiling, gasping for breath, groaning, sweating, and other physical manifestations are all too real."

Dr. Helen Wamback (1978) reports [6] "If my subjects were fantasizing, their fantasies were bleak and barren. The great majority of my subjects went through their lives wearing rough homespun garments, living in crude huts, and eating bland cereal grain with their fingers from wooden bowls".

---

[6] Wambach, Helen, PhD. Life After Life. 1978, Bantam Publishing New York, New York

According to Dr. Wambach's research of 1,088 cases, she found 10% of her regressed subjects lived upper class lives in each time period studied and 60 – 77% lived in the lower classes. She also found that the subjects that experienced the most happiness in their past lives lived as primitives or peasants. Additionally, Dr. Wambach found that 60% of her regressed subjects could answer her question about their purpose in incarnating: 18% came to be more social, 18% came so they could work out karmic relationships, 26% came to obtain new experience, 27% returned to help others or themselves grow spiritually, and 12% came for miscellaneous reasons. Her research also found that only 76% chose their sex and in 24% there was no choice or they were not aware of a choice.

The concept of reincarnation or the rebirth of the soul into successive bodies is a belief held by the majority of the world's Eastern Religions such as Hinduism, Buddhism, Sufism, Jaines, Jewish Cabbalists as well as the Theosophical Society and the Free Masons, some of whose members were among the founding fathers of the United States.

When an extensive United States Gallup Poll was taken using a population base of 166 million adults eighteen years or older in 1981, the finding showed that at least one quarter of the population polled believed in reincarnation.

Some of the most brilliant thinkers throughout time have become initiates to the doctrine of rebirth. Their writings are an inspiring legacy of wisdom to help inform us as to the process of reincarnation. We can count among these great teachers such names as Plato, Pythagoras, Origin, St Augustine, Goethe, Leonardo Di Vince, William Blake, Ralph Waldo Emerson, Wagner, Tolstoy, Benjamin Franklin, Walt Whitman, Gandhi, Jack London, Mark Twain, Sir Winston Churchill, Theologian Robert Graves, Norman Mailer, Herman Hesse, and General George Patton. Some examples are as follows:

"I know I am deathless. No doubt I have died myself ten thousand times before. I laugh at what you call dissolution, and I know the amplitude of time." Walt Whitman

"So as through a glass and darkly, the age long strife I see. Where I fought in many guises, many names, but always me." General George Patton

"As long as you are not aware of the continual law of Die and Be Again, you are merely a vague guest on a Dark Earth." Johann Wolfgang von Goethe

Benjamin Franklin, as a young man of twenty-two wrote his epitaph which reads:

The body of
B. Franklin, Printer
Like the cover of an Old book
Its contents torn out
And Stript of its Lettering and Guilding
Lies Here, Food for Worms.
But the Work shall not be Lost,
For it will (as he Believ'd) Appear once More
In a New and More Elegant Edition
Revised and Corrected
By the Author

Fredrich Nietzsche stated: "Live so that thou mayest desire to live again – that is thy duty – for in any case thou wilt live again."

Some individuals would say that humankind grasps for an explanation out of death, a way to evade a person's greatest fear. The theory of reincarnation offers hope and solace to those who wish to deliver themselves from the despair of the meaninglessness of life and the finality of permanent existence, but I offer perhaps it was not fear of death, but knowledge, insight and spiritual understanding that inspired such great philosophical thinkers.

Accounts of Reincarnation

While living in Virginia many years ago, I lived within walking distance to the small white frame Catholic Church where Clara Barton nursed the injured and dying civil war Union soldiers. Our five-acre property was once covered by a Union soldier encampment and the extensive trenches that snaked throughout the land were a grim reminder of history's haunting presence.

When my younger son was around four years old we would go on walks and he would point to the ground saying "me and David had to dig that trench". David was my son's best friend and he would often talk about what happened to them during the Civil War. My son currently has no past life recollections and no belief in reincarnation.

As a young child my son told the story of how his gun jammed during a battle and he was killed. In this lifetime, he attended gunsmith school and was obsessed for a short time with developing a smooth gun action that would not jam.

Sylvia Cranston and Carey Williams (1993) wrote about a mathematical genius named Shakuntala Devi in their book "Reincarnation".

Devi was born in India to an uneducated family, but at the age of three she could work out logarithms, roots and sums in minutes. Devi had little education and yet in 1977 she outperformed one of the Worlds' most advanced computers "figuring out the twenty third root of 201-digit number in less than fifty seconds, faster than the computer".

Devi believed the source of her talent came from a past life that she had experienced in Egypt. History has revealed the extraordinary mathematicians who once lived in the land of the Pharaohs.

There is also an astonishing story reported by Sylvia Cranston and Cary Williams (1993) [7]about an African American blind slave born in 1849 called "Blind Tom". The account was found in the Music Division of the Performing Arts Research Center at Lincoln Center in New York.

"The first amazing demonstration of Tom's musical virtuosity was the occasion when he, unexpectedly (at the age of three) joined his voice with those of the Bethune girls as they were singing on the verandah steps of their plantation one evening. It was not the melody that he carried, but the most difficult second part... He, spontaneously and perfectly, carried on to the end of the Song."

The next surprising exhibition was the following year when Tom was four and it was an evening when the young ladies had several hours of music at the piano. After they scattered to different parts of the house, they heard the music that they had played earlier being repeated on the piano. The women hastened back to the parlor to find the blind child at the keyboard playing back all the music that he had heard.

It was highly unlikely that a young blind slave boy would have received piano lessons or had access to a piano to practice in a busy white household. The young boy was also aware of major and minor scales and it was reported that young Tom "displayed an absolute accuracy of fingering which a highly professional reviewer in 1862 declared was "of the schools".

General Bethune the slave owner of young Tom, sought out a

---

[7]   Cranston, Sylvia. Reincarnation, A New Horizon In Science, Religion, and Society: 1993. Theosophical University Press, Pasadena, California

formal teacher for Tom, but when the teacher heard the boy play, he stated:[8]

"No sir, I give up; the world has never seen such a thing as this little blind Negro and will never see such other. I can't teach him anything, he knows more of music than we know or can learn – all that great genius can reduce to rule and put in tangible form: he knows more than I do; I don't even know what it is, bit I see and feel it is something beyond my comprehension."

The genius of Tom was well documented as he played concerts for thousands of soldiers fighting in the Civil War. Tom also played at the White House for President Lincoln. Tom's amazing life also speaks to the importance of a larger consciousness that is played out in community, state, country, and global levels. Throughout history, people have appeared to test our perceptions and present a reality check to wrong thinking.

---

[8]   Cranston, Sylvia. Reincarnation, A New Horizon In Science, Religion, and Society: 1993. Theosophical University Press, Pasadena, California

Cryptomnesia

D r. Reina Kampman, a Finnish psychiatrist believes reincarnation
memories are actually based on cryptomnesia, which is a fantasy
build around a severely disturbing event.

A good example of cryptomnesia would be a short story Helen
Keller wrote as a young teenager that was published. Later Ms. Keller
discovered her story had aspects similar to a story written by Margaret
Camby that was published in 1874.

Dr. Kampman would say Helen unconsciously used features "from
a book she had read has a child". Unfortunately, Ms. Keller was accused
of plagiarism. Perhaps Helen Keller was Margaret Camby in a past life
as they had many similarities.

There are also other theories to dispel reincarnation such as the
hypnotist "leaking" information to the hypnotized subject telepathically
or the subject gathering information from the Akashic records which
is considered to be a field where everything that has gone on in the
universe is mysteriously recorded.

Another explanation from the skeptics for past life memories is
that hypnotized subjects tell fantasies making up stories that have
more archetypal themes related to unconscious processes. This could
certainly be the case for subjects that are not deeply hypnotized. Also, I
have encountered individuals that have secrets they want to hide or are
afraid to actually delve into real problems so they make up stories about

being surrounded by angels, seeing themselves as royalty or having an unprecedented metaphysical experience.

It is easy to distinguish the fantasy from the true regression as the subject will ramble on embellishing their story and the deeply hypnotized person will generally be more precise with fewer words addressing only the images that come into their minds eye.

Another compelling feature that implicates reincarnation are the stories told of children speaking in languages they have had no exposure to or another phenomenon called "Sudden Accent Syndrome".

Sylvia Cranston (1993)[9] wrote about the story told by a well-known actor Melvyn Douglas. He reported that Robin Hull, a boy of five would produce what his mother thought were just strange sounds. As time when on, the child continued to use the strange utterances as if they had definite meaning.

At a dinner party, one of the Hull's guests was a woman who believed in reincarnation. She asked Mrs. Hull if she could bring a professor familiar with Asian languages to visit the boy.

After spending time with the boy, the professor reported to his mother that her son was talking in a dialect used in northern Tibet. No one in the family, or friends of the family spoke this language or had visited Tibet.

One of the most compelling arguments for reincarnation would be the instances of a condition called "Foreign Accent Syndrome".

Foreign Accent Syndrome was first addressed at the end of World War II when a Norwegian woman was hit in the head by shrapnel. She fell into a coma and when she woke up, she spoke with a strong German accent.

According to the Washington Post, sixty cases of Foreign Accent

---

[9]   Cranston, Sylvia. Reincarnation, A New Horizon In Science, Religion, and Society: 1993. Theosophical University Press, Pasadena, California

Syndrome have been reported worldwide. There is a report of an American man who spoke with a Southern accent all his life who after waking from a stroke began speaking with a proper British accent.

Another woman who was raised in Pennsylvania started speaking with a Russian accent after falling down a stairwell and hitting her head. Another woman from Louisiana, after having a brain injury, started speaking with a Cajun dialect.

Researchers and Neurologists look for a biological link to explain the syndrome, but it seems more likely the physical trauma actually triggered cellular memory from a past life.

Some clients I have worked with, while deeply hypnotized during a regression have answered my questions in a language that is foreign to them in their current life. Everything that we have experienced is stored somewhere within our cellular memory.

The energy of the soul develops its own personality dynamic which relies on and is referenced by our experience. Our personality is an accumulation of patterns, choices, preferences and abilities that emerge as a coherent sequel from one lifetime to the next. People, places, and environment might be changed like the settings of a stage, but the events string together in a cohesive adaption of cause and effect events.

The continuation of talents through reincarnation explains the phenomena of the prodigal child such as presented by such great masters like Mozart, Michelangelo, and Leonardo Di Vinci.

The important work of Dr. Ian Stevenson, who was a professor at the Medical School of University of Virginia in the department of Neurology and Psychiatry now deceased, brought us some of the most compelling research in the field of reincarnation investigation.

Dr. Stevenson worked specifically with spontaneous memories of recollected past lives, mostly collected from children. Based on their past life testimonials a fact finding investigation was mounted to ascertain the accuracy of the vivid recollections of their former lives.

One example of Dr. Stevenson's research was the accounting of a boy named Prakash, born in the town of Chhatta, India in 1951. He was the reincarnation of a ten-year-old boy named Nirmal who died in 1950 in a town named Kosi Kalan just six miles away from Prakash's home.

The young child Prakash during his early years would spend much of his time crying and by the age of four he was reported to run out of his home insisting he wanted to go home to Kosi Kalan. He would also insist that his name was Nirmal.

In 1961 the father of Nirmal came to visit Prakash at his home in Chhatta. The boy immediately recognized his father from a past life when he lived in Nirmal. Prakash's family then took him to visit Nirmal's family in Kori Kalan and the young boy wept when he was reunited with Nirmal's older sister. In addition, Prakash also knew details about people, places and personal effects that belonged to the deceased Nirmal.

While in Lebanon Dr. Stevenson was able to investigate the story of a boy before the different families got involved making this evidence very important as there was not outside interference.

The villagers from the town of Kornayel told Dr. Stevenson of a five-year-old boy named Imad Elawar who had talked about his former life since the age of one. The doctor was able to record over fifty items that the young boy remembered from his past life. The young child's first words were "Jamileh" and "Mahmound", which were people he knew from a past life. It turned out that Jamileh was his mistress in a former life and Mahmoud was his uncle. The boy revealed many facts about his past life. Dr. Stevenson took Imad and his father to his former home in a previous life where the boy recognized thirteen relatives and personal effects. When Imad was asked by his sister Huda what did he say before his death, Imad answered her saying, "Huda, call Fuad." The sister verified the answer was correct.

While facilitating past life regressions when I lived in Virginia, I worked with a woman who suffered from severe pain in her throat. She saw many doctors, but they were unable to cure her or find the root cause of her pain. Frustrated with her condition, the woman came to see me as a last resort. During her regression she told the story of being the son of a peasant who was unable to financially care for his son so he took him to live at a monastery where he would be fed, educated, and cared for.

It so happened that the boy had a beautiful voice and as was the custom of the church, the boy was prepared to be castrated so he could maintain his soprano voice. During the regression the woman cried out in pain as she became the boy in her mind's eye revisiting the past trauma. The boy was held down by the monks as a scalding poker was placed down his throat, soon after the boy fainted from the pain. During the time of unconsciousness, the boy was then castrated. The trauma that was most prominent with the boy and registered in the cellular memory was the cauterization of the throat as the young boy was awake during the incident.

A week after the regression, the woman reported that she had no more pain in her throat. I however, was a bit perplexed as the incident pertaining to the castration of the young boy did not make sense to my knowledge of history. Doing extensive research on the subject, I found that sometimes the monks would also singe the back of the throat along with castration. My client would have no way of knowing this information as she was not much of a reader or interested in history.

During my first personal past life regression facilitated by a well-known psychic in Virginia who also worked with the FBI, I saw myself as a young girl about the age of twelve or thirteen getting ready for an event. The year was 1421 and I was living within the castle walls with my family in Ireland. There was a large banquet and everyone was excited and making preparation. I could see myself putting on red slippers that matched the rich fabric of my high waisted dress. I also saw streams of bright red waves of hair and my father was a large round jolly man with the same red hair.

My mother appeared to be sterner with brown hair and a petite stature. We were going to a big feast and all my senses were alive with the smells of food, hay, and the dankness of the stone walls. There was merriment everywhere and I was playing with other children when horses and soldiers came charging into the main courtyard. Mayhem and blood was everywhere as the soldiers massacred the stunned crowd. I could feel the fear and the horror inside me, and then a sword pierced through my back. I found myself next in a confused state wondering the rolling countryside outside the castle, no longer in human form.

Locating a book in the library on early Irish history, it told of a siege led by a brother against his older brother in 1421. The book described how the Irish King was having a large banquet within the castle walls and that his jealous younger brother attacked the unsuspecting kingdom, killing all the people and easily taking the castle and the throne for himself. I had not heard of this story or studied Irish history at this point in my life, but it does explain why I am drawn to things Celtic.

Many children are also plagued by early childhood fears and phobias unrelated to any current life stimuli. There are also children convinced they are the wrong sex having memories of a previous life sexual orientation which feels more congruent with their mind. Science tells us this is a biological anomaly, but the decision for sexual orientation often takes place in the mind.

There are also children who suffer with congenital birth deformities that cannot be explained by genetics or environment.

I once worked with a young man who was born missing two thirds of his left arm. During a regression he revealed that he had been married in a past life to a woman he was deeply in love with. One

41

night he found out his wife was cheating on him and in a jealous rage he hit her. The blow was so severe it knocked her over causing his wife to hit her head on the corner of the bedroom dresser. She died almost instantly and the man fell into deep depression as well as regret over what he had done. He carried the guilt throughout that lifetime, even into his death and beyond. The arm that he was missing in this lifetime was the arm that he used to administer the fatal blow to his wife.

Dr. Ian Stevenson (1975) also reported:[10] "Children born with deformed limbs – or even without fingers, toes, and hands – have claimed to remember being murdered and state that the murderer had removed these fingers, toes, or hands during the killing".

This would seem a cruel fate for someone who fell prey to a murderer as they would have to live with a constant reminder in their present life of a past horror. However, since we are self-actualizing spiritual beings with cellular memory, such a dramatic trauma would have a tendency to carry forward into the next life.

Part of my work as a regression therapist has been working with young men who in their previous lives had been soldiers killed in wars such as World War II and Viet Nam. Often they would bare birthmarks where they had been shot. Some of the birthmarks would have a main center with smaller marks surrounding – much like the distribution of shrapnel.

Dr. Stevenson had also made studies of birthmarks. One such study was the case of Victor Vincent, a Tlingit Indian who lived on an island off Alaska.

Prior to Victor's death in 1946 he predicted that he would reincarnate as his favorite niece's son. Victor told her, "I hope I don't stutter as much as I do now. Your son will have these scars".

---

[10]   Stevenson, Ian MD. Cases of the Reincarnation Type.1975, University Press of Virginia. Charlottesville.

Victor showed his niece the scar on his back from a surgery and a scar on the base of the right side of his nose. He told his niece that she would know it was him when she saw the same scars on the son that would be born to her.

In 1947, the niece gave birth to a son who had the two identifying birth marks as predicted by her uncle. The birth marks where in the same shape and location as Victors. As the baby grew he also was reported to talk with a stutter, further proof of Victor's reincarnation.

Reincarnation allows us to follow an evolutionary spiritual path of the hero's journey on a quest to discover the chalice within or one's own spontaneous nature of the masculine merged with the feminine principles.

Joseph Campbell[11] (1989) writes in his book an "Open Life" that the meaning of the hero's journey in search of the grail "is finding the dynamic source in your life so that its trajectory is out of your own center and not something put on you by society". There is a wonderful Sanskrit Mantra which tells us with mystical direction where to find the seed of the soul. The Mantra is "Om Mani Padme Hum" which means the "Jewel is in the Lotus". Our exercise of free will can move us away in material longing or inward on our spiritual quest and progress is made on the divine adventure as long as the individual acquires characteristics that enable manifestation towards divine nature.

Reincarnation as seen through the Buddhist perspective teaches that it is our attachment to desires which divert us from our spiritual path in order to follow achievement, pleasure, or avoidance of pain and suffering. It is the simple urge of these desires that draw us back into the world of matter time and time again, as well as the karma we must fulfill. As we think it, so we create it.

---

[11] Campbell, Joseph. An Open Life: 1989, Harper and Row Publishers, New York, New York

Perhaps it is desire itself that is our external and internal foe. Our desires gnaw at us like an insatiable addiction which obscures and depletes our spiritual connection.

The Bhagavad-Gita states: 3:36-39

"Know that here in the world desire is your foe, all consuming, all sinful. As a fire is obscured by smoke, as a mirror by dust, and as an embryo by the womb, so is all this wisdom obscured by passion (desire)."

Karma

The orientation that provides the impetus for reincarnation is the law of Karma. Newton's third law of motion stated "for every action there is an equal and opposite reaction". A good example is that often four to six months after a person goes through an emotional upheaval in their lives, they will find themselves going through a physical illness. It often takes some time for the mental to manifest in the physical and often it would be too inconvenient to be ill at the time of the stress onset. Karma also has a delayed response mechanism which sometimes gives us an opportunity to learn the lesson without suffering from consequences of cause and effect. Karma is known as the "law of cause and effect", destiny determined by conduct, or simply just "life Lessons".

Many years ago in Arlington, Virginia I would attend a Sai Baba ashram where we would watch video lectures by the Yogi. During one of the lectures, Sai Baba used the analogy of life in the material world being like a movie. We could pick a comedy, tragedy, drama, love story – whatever journey best served our Karmic condition.

He also continued by saying we could not change our character in the movie as the scenes and script were already written. The good news is that we can actually change the type of movie we are acting in so we are not forced to live a lifetime as the victim acting in a depressing drama if that is the script that we are currently encountering.

Madame Blavatsky[12] (1888) wrote in her book page 171 of the "The Secret Doctrine":

> "Intimately, or rather indissolubly, connected with Karma is the law of rebirth, or of reincarnation of the personalities. The latter are like the various costumes and characters played by the same actor, which each of which that actor identifies himself and is identified by the public, for the space of a few hours.
>
> The inner or real man who personates those characters knows the whole time that he is Hamlet for the brief space of a few acts, which represent however, on a plane of human illusion the whole life of Hamlet. And he knows that he was, the night before, King Lear, the transformation in his turn of a still earlier preceding night; but the outer visible character is supposed to be ignorant of the fact."

However, as we play actors shifting roles from lifetime to lifetime, our characters are not random. The time span for our Karma or cause and effect will wait for the right alignment of conditions in which we will appear for our next role in order that the soul will be able to gain the most fulfillment from the needed response mechanism.

Karma may be enacted as a person who has lived a depraved lavish lifestyle in a past life would be reborn to a life of financial struggles and social hardships.

---

[12] Blavatsky, H.P. The Secret Doctrine. (1888) republished 1999, Theosophical University Press. Pasadena, California

Edgar Casey [13](1967), a world famous medium, talked about three different kinds of Karma in his book "On Reincarnation" which he termed "Symbolic Karma", "Organismic Karma" and "Boomerang Karma".

An example of Organismic Karma would be a woman who killed her baby in a past life would be unable to bear a child in the next, which might also include stillbirths or miscarriages. Abortion is not necessarily included depending on the intentions and awareness of the person.

Symbolic Karma would encompass using a symbolic meaning and making it the physical reality, such as someone who felt intellectually superior to most people would have a very low IQ in the next life.

Boomerang Karma occurs when you do something to someone else and it happens to you in your next life such as raping someone and then being the victim of rape in your current life. This however, is not the case of all rapes as in many cases it can also have to do with loosing and reclaiming personal power.

Choosing to be male or female often has to do with which part of the persona needs more balancing. Carl Young wrote[14] about the significance of the "Anima" or feminine part of the male consciousness and "Animus" or masculine part of the female needing to come into harmony for the individual to move on to "self-actualization" or a higher consciousness.

Karmic conditions will be created that will most benefit the lessons that need to be learned from a sexual orientation and that will also have an effect on gender.

---

[13] Casy, Edgar. On Reincarnation. 1967: Warner Books. New York, New York

[14] Jung, C.G.. Memories, Dreams, Reflections.1961.Random House, New York, New York

I once had a male regression client who was very handsome, successful, athletic, and enjoyed wearing expensive stylish women's clothing. We found that in a past life he was a woman placed in an arranged marriage to a very frugal, unattractive and demanding farmer who lived in the countryside beyond Paris, France. The wife worked very hard on the farm, was stuck in a loveless marriage, and dreamed of a life in Paris with beautiful clothing to wear.

In his current life, the woman who was treated as a second class citizen by her husband, decided to reincarnate as a handsome successful man who traveled and could afford all the things that he was not able to have in the past life as a farmer's wife. The life choice made perfect karmic sense. Wearing beautiful women's clothing for the man was a wish fulfillment from his life as the sad woman who eventually died working in her husband's fields from a heart attack.

Unfortunately, this man had been in therapy for years, suffering as the therapist tried to extinguish his odd hobby. The man felt himself a freak of nature and lived in shame with his dark secret. He came to get a regression reporting that he was having suicidal thoughts. The regression gave him answers and understanding about what triggered his behavior and so his shame and depression disappeared, leaving him guilt free to fulfill his desires and wear women's clothing in appropriate accepting environments.

Rimpoche Nawang Gehlet [15] in his insightful book "Good Life, Good Death" page 146 states:

> "There is no such thing as a dead person, only a
> dead body. My consciousness, which came from a past
> life, remains in my present life and will travel through

---

[15] Rimpoche Nawang Gehlek. Good Life, Good Death. 2001. Riverhead Books: New York, New York

to my future life, without identity unless I am a highly developed practitioner: without memory".

Rimpoche Gehlek also states: "The Karma, or pattern of action, you create becomes an imprint, which travels with you."

Yale scientists Harold Saxton Burr and F.C. Northrop presented a paper after four years of research to the National Academy of Science. Their research proved that there was an electrical phenomenon that accompanied all growth which they termed "the electrical architect". The scientists were able to establish patterns or specific characteristics for each species that were recorded through the use of electrocardiographs and electroencephalographs.

Their hypothesis continues to point out that there is an electrical architect that exists in the bodies of living things and adheres to a specific predetermined pattern remaining as a constant force until death of the body. Kirlian photography proves that there is an energetic field that is attached to living things.

Unfortunately, the important research of Burr and Northrop has been mostly overlooked by researchers in favor of genetics. Pharmaceutical companies have had a large influence on the development of research as they want to reduce natural processes to chemical control and disregard or ignore the complexity of the human dynamic.

Gina Germinara who wrote "Many Mansions" recorded a statement made by Edgar Cayce during one of his channeled trance states:

> "The entity was not born merely by chance. For the earth is a causation world; cause and effects are in the earth a natural law. And as each soul enters this material plane, it is to meet or give these truths so that

others, too, may gain more knowledge of the purpose for which each soul enters.

You, in the beginning, had companionship with God, losing that companionship by choice of that which would satisfy material desire only. Thus you, as the Master (Jesus) did, enter again and again; you come to fulfill the law, the law that brought your soul into being to be one with Him."

Cayce continued: "You don't go to heaven; you grow to heaven!"

Reincarnation in Christianity

I was very lucky to be able to experience many different spiritual orientations and teachings while living in Santa Fe, New Mexico. I studied Buddhism with Lamas and Rinpoches, I explored Shamanism with Shamen from Peru, Brazil, Native America and I was a fifteen-year devotee of Ammachi from India, who was often called the hugging Yogi by the news media. In addition, I was privileged to attend lectures by Stanislav Grof, Mary Ann Williamson, Ram Das, Amit Gowsami, and many other great philosophical thinkers that arose out of the sixties metaphysical movement.

While my friends in Santa Fe enjoyed liberal lifestyles and a cornucopia of spiritual ideologies, many of them had a strong aversion to the "J" word. Some of my friends and acquaintances were recovering Catholics trying to erase the religion of guilt and many others rejected the blame and shame dogma of the traditional church and unfortunately placed the blame on Jesus.

After writing a book on early Christianity which took three years of research, I found the dogma was not part of Jesus' teachings, but that of the early Orthodox Church which later became the Catholic Church. I was elated to see that Jesus actually taught about reincarnation and Karma. Now I have had ministers tell me when Jesus talks about reincarnation, he is speaking in metaphor; he does not mean what he says literally. I am confused, because we must be careful about how we interpret biblical passages as often what is said is what is meant. Clearly I believe that both levels of metaphor and literal interpretation exist throughout the bible along with a historical/social perspective, but I think it is important to address the issues posed by the Christian churches against reincarnation. Jesus included reincarnation and Karma in his teachings, the Catholic Church removed the concept for a more lucrative endeavor.

The mention of reincarnation is a point of departure for many Christians as the Catholic Church removed reincarnation from the Christian doctrine between the third century and fifth century's movement to unite Christianity under one Catholic Church. The process started with the council of Nicene arranged by the Emperor Constantine in an attempt to have more control of the people by gathering them in one religion and then placing that church under the Emperor's rule.

Constantine was a pagan who worshiped one divinity, the "Sun God". He also had an interest in Christianity and kept by his side a Christian counselor, Bishop Hosius of Cordova. When Emperor Constantine fell desperately ill in April 337 he asked Bishop Eusebius to baptize him before his death. Constantine, knowing that he committed many sins sought baptism at his death in order that he would receive redemption just in case there was a heaven with the Christian God. Basically, he wanted all his bases covered for his journey to the next world.

Constantine marched on the city of Rome in October of 312 in order to confront Maximentius for power over the western half of the Roman Empire. After defeating Maximentius, the new Emperor Constantine was faced with an empire filled with diverse religions, quarreling people and a decaying pagan structure. The majority religion in Rome was now Christian do impart to the charity and generosity shown by the Gnostic communities to the Roman people suffering from the infrastructure deterioration of a declining empire. Christianity however, was fragmented into many different sects each having their own views about the teachings of Jesus as well as the divinity of Jesus. Constantine believed if the Roman Empire was to survive, it would need to be unified under one common religion and that would need to be organized under one common doctrine.

There is a story told that Constantine had a dream during his march to Rome in which Jesus appeared to him. Christ showed Constantine the sign of the Cross and told him to have his soldiers inscribe the sign on their standards instead of their old pagan symbols. The battle with Maximentius went quickly and easily in favor of Constantine's troops. Constantine was keenly aware of the power inherent within the Christian faith.

The Christian movement had suffered more than two hundred and fifty years of martyrdom at the hands of the Romans. Large scale persecutions began in the year 64 AD when the Emperor Nero blamed the Christians for the year's great fire which destroyed much of Rome.

In 62AD James the Just, brother of Jesus, a disciple of Jesus and a high priest of the temple in Jerusalem was stoned to death after an assembly of Sanhedrin charged him with "breaking the law". The charges were unjustly brought against James by another high priest Ananus because of jealousy.

James the Just is said to have written the First Apocalypse of James and it is said that he was given authority over the twelve disciples of Jesus in the early church. James and the other disciples of Jesus were practicing Jews who believed Jesus to be the "Messiah" and fulfillment of the Jewish prophecies. They also believed in reincarnation as part of their Jewish religious heritage.

After the death of James, there was a Jewish uprising against the Romans which eventually ended with Jerusalem destroyed and many of the remaining Jews following Christ's teachings fleeing to Antioch and

Alexandria where there were already established Jewish communities. From this time forward, thanks to the hard work and devotion of the disciples, Mary Magdalene, Peter, Matthias, Thomas, Simon, Jude, John, James, and many other followers of Jesus, the teachings of self-experience and self-revelation spread throughout Europe, parts of Asia and the Middle East.

The belief in reincarnation, in one form or another had been around for thousands of years. The Jewish mystics believe in the concept as well as the Essenes, the Platonists, indigenous cultures and most of the Eastern religions. According to Wikipedia, a gallop poll which was taken in 2005 states that 20% of adults living in the United States believe in reincarnation. Most important to Christianity, Jesus taught about reincarnation.

In the Gospel of John 17: 10-13 Jesus speaks to his disciples about reincarnation when they question the prophecy that says Elijah will return before the Messiah appears.

"And his disciples asked him, why then do the scribes say that Elijah must come first? Jesus answered, saying to them, Elijah will come first so that everything might be fulfilled.

"But I say to you, Elijah has already come, and they did not know him, and they did to him whatever they pleased. Thus also the Son of Man is bound to suffer from them.

And the disciples understood that what he had told them was about John the Baptist."

Interestingly, Jesus also taught that who lived by the sword will die by the sword, which is the concept of "cause and effect" or Karma. The story of Elijah makes a perfect case for the law of cause and effect.

Recorded in the Old Testament in Kings is the story of Elijah the prophet. Like John the Baptist, Elijah was hairy and dressed in animal skins. Elijah also came from the wilderness making announcements of impending calamity to the non-believers.

According to the scriptures, the Jewish people had once again turned to pagan Gods during the reign of King Ahab. Ahab's wife Jezebel ordered that all the prophets of God be executed.

Elijah proposed a public contest to King Ahab in order to establish with the people if the pagan god Baal or the God of Israel was stronger. For days and nights the prophets of Baal prayed, danced, jumped upon the alter and self-mutilated to no avail as Baal did not answer them.

When Elijah's turn came, he calmly prepared the alter with wood and bullock. Elijah then had the people dose the alter with twelve jars of water and at once a fire came and consumed everything. The people once again returned to their God of Israel and Elijah slaughtered the 450 priests of Baal by beheading them against God's will. The angry Queen Jezebel ordered Elijah to be beheaded in return, however, Elijah escaped.

Elijah had escaped beheading in that life only to be beheaded as John the Baptist as retribution for the beheading of the priests of Baal. It was not the judgment of God, but the law of cause and effect that was enacted.

Matthew 16:13 makes another pertinent reference to reincarnation when Jesus spoke to his disciples. "Who do men say that the Son of Man is? And they said, "Some say John the Baptist, others say Elijah, and others Jeremiah or one of the prophets".

It appears that the people and the disciples are expecting the physical return of dead prophets when the answer was given to Jesus. If they did not believe in reincarnation, their reply would have made no sense.

Jesus states in John 5:24; "Truly, truly, I say to you, he who hears my word and believes him who has sent me has everlasting life; and he does not come before the judgment, but he passes from death to life". Jesus continues in John 5:29 "And they will come out; those who have done good works to the resurrection of life; and those who have done evil works to the resurrection of judgment".

Judgment is not something placed on us by a judgmental and wrathful god. Judgment is the cosmic law of cause and effect. Whatever thoughts, words and deeds that we put into motion, those are the actions that we will cause for ourselves. Jesus was not threatening us but warning us. The resurrection of judgment is our return to a material world of desires in order to play out our karma. Resurrection of life is to be joined with the cosmic energetic Christ, creator, God or consciousness principle depending on your religious orientation.

Jesus also warns us about the wrath of God which is judgment as defined in John 3:36 as he tells us; "He who believes in the Son has eternal life" (of the spirit) and he who does not obey the Son shall not see life, but the wrath (judgment) of God shall remain on him". The judgment will continue to stay with the person until they free themselves from judgment through right action.

Jesus further teaches of the law of cause and effect in Luke 7:37 – 38:

> *"Judge not, and you will not be judged; condemn not, and you will not be condemned; forgive, and you will be forgiven.*
>
> *Give, and it will be given to you: good measure shaken down and running over they will pour into your robe. For with the measure that you measure, it will be measured to you."*

Jesus tells us that he is "the way and the truth and the life". Clearly Jesus came to this world to reunite us with spirit, turn us from worldly entrapments and teach us how to live the spiritual life. This is the life Jesus speaks about in the Gospels. Jesus is the way, God is the truth, and the life is the spirit. Again, we refer back to the journey of the soul to understand our earthly existence as devised through the creation of free will.

The Gospel of Thomas addresses reincarnation in the fourth stanza: "Jesus said, *"The man old in days will not hesitate to ask a small child seven days old about the place of life and he will live. For many who are first will become last, and they will become one and the same."*

The Soul has come as an emissary or emanation of spirit into a physical manifestation in order to have experience in the world of matter and forgets its heavenly origins. The soul is part of the spirit and yet the spirit exists separate from the soul. Jesus was a spiritual being emanated from God and was sent to earth to bring us to awareness of our spiritual roots. Through Jesus we are taught and shown the way of spirit in order that we are able to remember our divine origins, evolve through free will into our spiritual nature, and reunite with God or the Supreme Being; however, we want to identify the cosmic consciousness.

It is important to understand the nature of existence in order to treat any malady of the physical/mental disorder. Through the journey of reincarnation and Karma we know that if someone has been a murderer in one life they might be murdered in the next life. If someone has been jealous and manipulative in one life, they might be the brunt of the same behavior in another life. And if someone has been kind, generous and compassionate in a past life, they have the option of returning to help aid others less fortunate to migrate to their spiritual awakening.

Jesus also instructs that the measure of a person is formed in the heart. Luke 7:45 "A good man brings out good things from the good treasure of his heart; and a bad man from the bad treasure of his heart brings out bad things for from the abundance of the heart the lips speak."

Jesus warns that we cannot say one thing from our mouth, that we do not believe in our hearts as incongruence causes internal conflict and it is what is registered in the heart that has the effect in our life. I have found that when people do not express their true feelings, hold resentments or guilt, it causes energetic blocks in the mind and body which often leads to illness. Repressed energy is always registered in cellular memory so it can sit dormant until triggered at a later date. Symptoms of trauma are also constructs of cellular memory.

There is such a thing as cellular memory which compels us to act and feel in unconscious ways. It is actually the souls' way of self-actualizing as it brings into conscious awareness those things that have carried over from unconscious processes due to trauma, ignorance, guilt, and our own self-judgment. It is through the process of bringing present the unconscious material that we try to resolve the inconsistencies of the soul.

Reincarnation explains the inequities and injustices that are apparently stark between individuals. One person is born to a life of poverty and despair while another person is born into a life of privilege. However, one must be careful not to assume that the more spiritually aligned person would be the privileged individual.

For hundreds of years, theologians have dismissed the importance of reincarnation saying that it is important to focus on the life we are currently living. This is absolutely true, and if we could each live a spiritual life as directed by the masters, we would be able to absolve any Karmic debt. Unfortunately, many of us have a difficult time with discernment or our attachment to desires which keeps us spiritually going around in a Karmic dance of circles like whirling dervishes.

One of the most important writers and orators on early Christianity was born in Alexandria, Egypt around the year 185 AD as there are differing dates. His name was Origen[16] and his parents were both

---

[16] Origin (2012). In Encyclopaedia Britannica.Retieved from http://www.britannica.com/EB checked topic/432455/Origin

martyrs of the Christian movement. Origen was a brilliant scholar devoted to scriptural authority until his martyred death in 250 AD by the Catholic Church. Many early Christians looked to Origin as a source of legitimate Christian thought pertaining to the meaning of the many Christian gospels.

Origin wrote commentaries to establish his thesis on the pre-existence and fall of souls, the transmigration of souls and the eventual restoration of all souls to a state of dynamic perfection in relation to a God-head.

Refinus's Latin translation of Origen's writing[17] "de Principiis, Bk. III, sec 4 cites the somewhat watered down statement by Origen on reincarnation:

> "Rational creatures had also a similar beginning. Indeed, if they had a beginning such as the end for which they hope, they must have unquestionably existed from the very beginning of the ages which are not seen... if this be so, then of course there has been a descent from a higher to lower condition not only by those souls who have deserved this change by the variety of their inner movements of consciousness, but also by those who in order to serve the world, came down from the higher and invisible spheres to these lower visible ones."

In 553 AD the writings of Origen were declared heresy by the Church and one of the major controversies was around his teachings on reincarnation. The criticisms over reincarnation were first started

---

[17]   Origin. De Principiis, Bk.III, section 4

during the first Council of Nicea. Many early church organizers could not reconcile themselves to the evidence that Jesus clearly left for them.

Theophilus, patriarch of Alexandria (385-412 AD) argued in the Jerome letters 98:11:

> "What is the point of preaching that souls are repeatedly confined in bodies, only to be released again, and that we experience many deaths? Does he (Origen) not know that Christ came, not in order to free souls from bodies after their resurrection or to clothe freed souls in bodies once again that they might come down from heavenly regions to be invested once again with flesh and blood? Rather, he came so that he might present our revived bodies with incorruptibility and eternal life."

Essentially, the church was saying that people should try and live by the teachings of Jesus, but in case they do not, they can go to Jesus via the Church and have their sins taken away. How much would a dying person pay to have their sins relieved? The answer might shed some insight on the considerable wealth of the Catholic Church.

The Catholic Church developed five major points against reincarnation as being part of Christianity.

1. It seems to minimize Christian salvation.
2. It is in conflict with the resurrection of the body.
3. It creates an unnatural separation between body and soul.
4. It is built on a much too speculative use of Christian scriptures.
5. There is no recollection of previous lives.

In answer to the Catholic Churches criticisms, I have certainly met many individuals who have spontaneous memories of past lives, including myself. Dr. Ira Stevenson at the University of Virginia has collected excellent data and written volumes about spontaneous reincarnation memories of children from around the world.

Knowing that I will have to pay retribution for my wrongful acts really keeps me on the straight and narrow. I truly accept the Karmic law of cause and effect, and so I work persistently at not sowing any seeds that I do not want to reap.

As far as the Church's accusation of speculation of scripture, it seems Jesus was pretty clear about reincarnation when he said that John the Baptist was Elijah.

Additionally, the charge of creating an unnatural state between body and soul seems to miss the very point of Jesus teachings, his death and resurrection. The body was made as a temple to house the soul so it can have an experience in the world of matter. Jesus said in Matthew 17: 15-16: "For whoever wishes to save his life shall lose it; and whoever loses his life for my sake shall find it. For how would a man be benefited, if he should gain the whole world and lose his own soul?"

Jesus is telling us that one must die to the ego and attachment to the material world in order to engage ones' soul and move into Christ energy. The material body and the soul are not one in the same, but rather a harmonizing system of form and spirit. The form will return to the earth elements from where it came and the spirit or energy system will continue on its spiritual path towards its origins.

For many years I have facilitated past life regressions and rarely do I give a directive to anyone to go to a past life as I feel that would be leading them to an area that was from my will instead of their will. During all that time, I have not found one person who in a state of deep hypnosis, did not eventually go into a past life whether they believed in reincarnation or not.

One of the most interesting developments from my regression work is to realize the people I have regressed lived past lives as both male and female, have been many different races, and have participated in many different cultures as well as religions. This awareness gets to the heart of Jesus' teaching "love one another" because in essence we are one another.

The doctrine of reincarnation asserts that there is a cosmic drama which accounts for the individual soul that provides conditions for its self-actualization or return to spiritual awakening. This concept exerts that through a series of Karmic lessons (cause and effect) the soul which is compelled into the world of matter forgetting its spiritual nature, will encounter experience in the world of suffering, joy and free will.

In actuality the soul being is multidimensional. Quincy Howe, Jr. wrote in his book "Reincarnation For The Christian" (p 82): explaining;[18]

> "Our traditional Christian view of creation envisions God fashioning the Cosmos out of the void, something alien to himself. There is already a rather troublesome contradiction here, in the void (which is by definition empty) is providing the stuff of creation."

Christian theologian Origen also wrote in "de Principus":

> "Every soul...comes into the world strengthened by the victories or weakened by the defeats of its previous life. Its pace in the world as a vehicle appointed to honor or dishonor is determined by its

---

[18] Howe, Quincy. Reincarnation For The Christian. 1974. Westminster Press, Philadelphia, Pennsylvania

previous merits or demerits. Its work in this world determines its place in the world which is to follow."

Justinian, the Roman Emperor in 593 AD and a group of Orthodox Christian leaders declared war on reincarnation and its Christian believers. Hans Ptolzere, author of "Patterns of Destiny wrote: "The Church needed the whip of judgment day to keep the faithful in line. It was therefore a matter of survival for the Church not to allow belief in reincarnation to take hold among her followers."

The Catholic Church under Justinians's rule murdered millions of Christians and almost completely wiped out the Gnostic sects of Christianity. The Cathars in Europe who were another Christian sect that believed in reincarnation were also almost extinguished by the Church in the Middle Ages, uprooting any thoughts of reincarnation from public awareness.

Thankfully, Paramahanso Yogananda, a Yogi from India came to the United States in 1920 bringing with him the philosophy of Yoga, the tradition of meditation and the doctrine of reincarnation as found in the Rig Vedas. Europe also had the mystical writings of Madame Blatvinsky and Alice Baily, whose teachings were made more accessible by Torkom Saraydarian covering the idea of reincarnation and the journey of the soul.

Also, due to the unfortunate circumstance which caused the evacuation of the Dali Lama from Tibet, Tibetan Buddhism is now practiced around the world. Few Westerners have not at least encountered some of the basic principles and teachings of the Buddha which includes mindfulness of what we say and do trying to do "no harm" to ourselves or others, non-attachment to the material world which helps us learn the wisdom of "emptiness" and without wisdom and non-attachment we will be stuck in the cyclic existence of reincarnation and Karma.

Currently, we are fortunate to live in an age where the bridge between science and consciousness is narrowing. What many religions teach us, Quantum Physics scientifically is beginning to demonstrate as it is consciousness that has brought us science and not the other way around. It is our current inability to interpret the dynamic field of information that causes the disconnect in what we chose to accept.

Quantum Physics, The Case For Reincarnation

Einstein taught the world that all matter is combined with energy when he formulated the equation E=Mc square. Einstein opened the door to a new science called Quantum Physics and gave us a leap in human understanding of what is reality.

When famous quantum physicist Amit Goswami was addressed in an interview by Connie Hill pertaining to the mutual exclusiveness of science and spirituality, Dr. Goswami made a profound statement.[19]

"The division happened because of a quirk of history: that classical physics was discovered before quantum physics. If quantum physics had been discovered first, we would not have these separations between science and spirituality. Carl Popper coined the phrase "promissory materialism". Materialism will always remain promissory in those areas of spirit, soul and mind, meaning and what life is all about. Science based on materiality will never make total sense. It first has some questions that have a reductive tendency. Some things we do are materially oriented. If you need a job you learn a skill. But on the other hand if you want to be happy, to think money or work will make us

---

19   Hill, Connie. "An Interview With Amit Goswami". September 2002. Living Now.

happy is foolhardy. One becomes happy by connecting with wholeness. This wisdom has escaped most scientists."

One of the amazing discoveries made by physicists was that if you continually break matter into smaller pieces to the point you are down to electrons and protons, you will find they no longer possess the traits of the objects. This means that scientists have found electrons are without dimension.

Additionally, physicist found that an electron can manifest as a wave which spreads out over space or a particle which appears like a tiny spark of light when it strikes a surface.

Light, X-rays, radio waves and gamma rays can change from waves to particles and back again, which proves that our world of matter is just an illusion.

In order for physicists to classify waves and particles which are ever changing, they call them quanta and it is quanta that are the basic stuff which makes up the universe.

Ernest Holmes addressed the issue of mass and energy when he stated:[20] "It was only during the last few years of Einstein's life that this foremost scientist came to the general conclusion that there was no such thing as mass and that we could, in a more abstract way, resolve all things into pure energy".

In agreement with Einstein, the Physicist Bohr concluded that twin particles are part of an indivisible system and the subatomic particles do not exist until they are observed. This refers back to the spiritual system of what we think and say creates our reality.

A good example of people creating their reality is the simple idea of the placebo effect. There are always a percentage of people who become well when given placebos by doctors or researchers. This is because

---

[20] Homes, Earnest. The Infinite Concept of Cosmic Creation. 1956. Unarius. E Cajon, California

the placebo actually tricks the person into believing they are given a medicine to make them well. The person responds to their belief system and actually taps into their own healing forces within their psyche to heal themselves.

An interesting story is noted in the book "The Holographic Universe" (p.105)[21] by Michael Talbot. The author tells the true story about a boy suffering from a very serious hereditary condition known as Brocq's disease. The illness causes the skin to develop a thick horny covering resembling the scales of a reptile. The skin becomes hard and brittle, cracking and bleeding with the slightest movement causing serious infections and shortened life spans.

A hypnotist at the Queen Victoria Hospital in London found that by taking the boy into a deep hypnotic trance and using hypnotic suggestions the boy was able to completely cure himself of his infirmary.

During the past fifteen years I have worked as a regression therapist and have personally witnessed the amazing power people have within themselves to cure serious illnesses, mental afflictions and simple neurotic habits. I never doubt the power of the mind and spirit working in concert to elevate and improve the nature of human potential.

Another important quantum physicist by the name of Dr. Bohm[22] theorized that without an observer, particles such as electrons do not exist. Bohm decided there must be a field that pervaded all of space which he termed "Quantum Potential". This field was different than magnetic fields and gravity fields because it did not diminish with distance, but maintained a subtle, equally powerful field everywhere.

Another important finding of quantum physics is that researchers

---

21   Talbot, Michael. The Holographic Universe, 1991: Harper Collins Publisher, New York, New York.

22   Schwartz, Gary, Ph.D. The Living Energy Universe. 1999 Hampton Roads Publishing, Charlottesville, Virginia

have found at least ten dimensions. This accounts for the different realms that Jesus, Buddhists, Sufi's, Hindus and many other religions speak about. I believe that the destruction that humans manifest is not localized to the earth, but has far reaching consequences on a multi-dimensional level. Teilhard De Chardin[23] believed that the physical body was a microcosm of the entire universe and that the Universe is a living conscious being. Chardin stated: "We are not human beings having a spiritual experience, we are spiritual beings having a human experience".

Several years ago I attended a lecture by Dr. Amit Goswami. Many people know of him from the movie about consciousness called "What the Bleep". This film helps to visually illustrate the idea of quantum physics in our everyday life. I was very excited to hear a revered physicist expanding the world of science to include the spiritual dimension. Dr. Goswami theorizes that "consciousness is the ground of all being".

Dr. Goswami (p.14) further states that;[24] "Observation by a conscious observer is responsible for the wave function collapse in quantum mechanics". The theory is important because it says consciousness is related to the creation of reality as first suggested by the seventeenth century Anglo-Irish Philosopher Bishop Berkely. The idea is that whatever the majority of thoughts that are being thought in the world at any given time create the reality of it. And of course, as there are many different thoughts, we create many different realities from a war raging in the Middle East due to fear and imperialism to a peaceful communal tribe living in the South American Rain Forest.

How quantum physics relates to the issue of trauma and methods

---

[23]   Dde Chardin Teilhard. The Phenomenon Of Man. 1976: Harper Publishing, New York, New York

[24]   Goswami. Amit Ph.D. Physics of the Soul. 2001, Hampton Roads Publishing, Charlottesville, Virginia

to heal trauma demonstrates for us that the medical model is only a secondary response system as doctors speculate on the biological effects of the world of matter. Illness, whether manifested in the physical or mental form, often has its origins at a more temporal level. Our ability to heal ourselves relates back to delays or interruptions in the "feedback loop", or in layman terms, mind over matter.

On December 19, 2009 "The Wichita Eagle" a newspaper out of Kansas reported a story about a man lifting a car off a six-year-old girl to save her life. The man was only 5'7" and weighed 185 pounds when he somehow found enough strength to lift a Mercury sedan off the child who was pinned under the car.

One is compelled to go back to the basic concepts of physics developed by Albert Einstein in order to address the physics of reincarnation. E=mc square tells us that matter can be turned into energy and energy into matter. Energy and matter are symbiotic systems in time space reality or the spiritual energetic being entwined within the physical vehicle contained in the world of matter.

The law of general covariance as listed in Wikipedia states; "the laws of physics should take the same form in all coordinate systems". The implications of this statement on a spiritual level would mean that we cannot confine our view of who we are to a physical time space reality as we are also energetic beings and part of a grand cosmic energetic principle which can be referred to as cosmic consciousness or from a religious perspective "God".

Science wants to stick to the facts and yet in some scientist's narrow minded tunnel vision they overlook so many facts. Hypotheses are judged by outcome. Can we not understand reincarnation and past life regression from the stand point of outcomes based on qualitative facts? How can one view the galaxies and beyond and still feel any sense of biological empiricism? As a small child I would gaze at the sky and loose myself within the vastness of the stars and space. My mind would become dizzy and disoriented as I felt lost in my reflections of an unknown Universe.

Eugene Wigner[25], winner of the 1963 Nobel Prize in physics and a man of great intellect shared his view when he stated; "Man may have a nonmaterial consciousness capable of influencing matter."

My Buddhist teacher would confound me when she would say "you are not the actual being, but the caretaker of the actual being."

This statement took me into deep contemplation and research. I found that as Dr. Wigner had asserted, there is a presence that acts as spectator and guide that is me, but not me. There is the existence of a non-material conscious mind that is linked to me and to an all permeating field of consciousness.

---

[25] Nouenberg, Michael. (2007) "Quantum Enigma, Physics Encounters Consciousness", Aug 2007, Springer Science and Business Media, LLC.

Biology Versus Mind

M uch like the age old question of "nature versus nurture" we must also address the question "biology versus spirituality". Is it the biology that drives the function of the human dynamic or the energy linked to our spiritual source that is our dominant orientation?

Many years ago as an undergraduate in psychology I was unlucky enough to have a professor who believed only in nurture and taught his class on his premise. Six months prior to starting my sociology class I had just given birth to my second child and found the very question of "nature versus nurture" to be ridiculous. There are few mothers in the world who would not tell you how different their children are from one another. Even in-utero babies develop their own personality characteristics.

One child can be strong and constantly moving, while another is quiet and passive. Of course, one must factor in the mental/physical state of the mother during the pregnancy which does have an effect on the child, as nature and nurture are both significant factors in the development of a child. As an example of children having their own personalities without interference from the parents, I have several friends who had children that refused to eat meat from a very young age even though they were not raised in vegetarian households.

I would not retract for this professor, what I knew to be true so

I had to withdraw from the class in order to save myself from being failed.

The biological medical model has much the same attitude. If you do not agree with the prevailing mentality of scientific thought, you are dismissed by them. There is no room for legitimate inquiry that might interfere with their fixed belief systems. However, like my old professor, old paradigms of science will eventually find their theories to be limited and short sighted.

While I believe firmly that the human condition develops both from nature and nurture, I also believe that we are a product of biology and spirit. In order to treat trauma, we must treat the mind, body and spirit connection because trauma is registered in all three orientations.

One could argue that this was a theological debate not rooted in science; however, the healthcare profession has challenged the very foundations of the concepts of spiritual nature by the developing field of biochemistry and pharmacology.

While researchers fixate on neurotransmitters, receptors, neurons, and brain chemistry, Dr. Merzeneich[26] was performing research to conclude that the brain was "plastic" or dynamic in nature. Many neuroscientists were focused on the idea that the brain was dictated by localization. This was the viewpoint that we are born with a "hardwired" system or maps which dictate how the brain represents the body and the world. If the system is "hardwired" who is doing the "hardwiring"?

Norman Doidge, M.D. (p. 169) writes about processes of the brain and how it functions during a feedback loop:[27]

"Normally, when we make a mistake, three things happen. First,

---

[26]   Doidge, Norman M.D. The Brain That Changes Itself. 2007. The Penguin Group. New York, New York

[27]   Doidge, Norman, M.D.. The Brain That Changes Itself. 2007: Penguin Group, New York, New York.

we get a "mistake feeling", that nagging sense that something is wrong. Second, we become anxious and that anxiety drives us to correct the mistake. Third, when our brain allows us to move on to the next thought or activity. Then both the "mistake feeling" and the anxiety disappear."

What happens when the process is interrupted or as one might say "the gears get stuck" such as seen with trauma victims where they did not have the option or opportunity to correct the mistake? Are they doomed to be stuck in the second phase of anxiousness and anxiety?

Cognitive behaviorists believe that by changing the behavior pattern you are able to change the response. This sounds good in theory; however, the change needs to occur with regard to the original trauma whether in real or imagined time. Often dramas are created similar to the original trauma as a way to give the individual the ability to re-enact the scene so they can facilitate empowerment and healing. Unfortunately, often one just gets caught in the unfinished feedback loop moving psychologically like a hamster running on a wheel in a cage, never getting anywhere.

Robert Gottesman talks about the brain's biochemicals as the "information molecules" using a coded language to communicate with the body-mind network and theorizes[28] "that information transcends time and space, placing it beyond the confining limits of matter and energy".

Researcher Gregory Bateson talks about the[29] (p.257) "feedback loop" making the consciousness of the observer an important part of the perception of reality on a given situation. He uses the metaphor

---

[28] Doidge, Norman, M.D.. The Brain That Changes Itself. 2007:Penguin Group, New York, New York

[29] Pert, Candace. Ph.D.. Molecules of Emotion. 1997. Scribner: New York, New York

of a "cow grazing in a meadow and a botanist strolling through the same meadow," while both perceive the grass as green, the cow and the botanist will find different meaning in their experience.

Who is in charge of steering the ship or driving the vehicle which is our human form when the level of consciousness of the captain informs the brain what psychological changes to make?

Gregory Bateson defined information as "the difference that makes a difference". Adding the observer to the equation of defining reality we now must consider the consciousness of the observer. When trauma happens to a child such as sexual abuse, the ability of the child to observe with a logical mind has not yet been developed. There are many stories of children watching from out of their bodies or from the ceiling of the room as they are being attacked. Somehow the spiritual body separated from the physical body as the rape occurred as a way to lessen the impact of the trauma.

When my friend and professional psychologist was attacked and robbed while traveling through Peru, her heightened state of consciousness allowed her to deal with her unfortunate situation and not fragment from the reality of the situation. While very shaken up, she was still able to move on to the next step which was getting help and replacing her money as well as her passport.

Dr. Edith Pert makes the analogy about how a feedback loop works in her book "Molecules Of Emotion", stating:[30]

"And the same principle functions to the psychosomatic network which is analogous to a boat sailing along as a result of a series of feedback loops. Cells are constantly signaling other cells through the release of neuropeptides which bind with receptors. The signaled cells, like the helmsman or the sail trimmer, respond by making physiological

---

[30] Pert, Candace.Ph.D. Molecules of Emotion. 1997. Scribner: New York, New York

changes. These changes then send feedback information to the peptide secreting cells, telling them how much less or how much more of the peptide to produce. This is how the body and the sailboat move forward, through a series of rapid feedback loops".

Mentally and physically healthy people have rapid and unimpeded feedback loops allowing them to navigate their experiences with relative ease. Individuals who have suffered trauma often suffer problems and interruptions in their feedback loops causing physical and mental problems as their brain chemistry tries to adjust. I have worked with teens and adults who during a counseling session, when asked specific questions pertaining to something related to their trauma have fallen immediately asleep as if they have narcolepsy. They could not complete their feedback loop.

Again and again as psychologists, doctors and counselors, we are given proof that the human mind/body system is fluid and dynamic in nature.

There is also a coded system of messages hardwired into our cells called "information molecules" which communicate with the mind/body network. Part of this coded system implants historical trauma whether suffered on an individual basis or cultural basis. This makes the perfect case for past life trauma being experienced in present time.

The idea of the "information molecules" also explains déjà vu and why individuals feel emotionally connected to things they have no prior experience with. While traveling throughout Scotland, every time I heard bagpipes at sunset tears would start to flow down my cheeks. I don't even really like the sound of bagpipes and yet the sound touched me somewhere deep in my soul and a feeling of sadness would pour over me. I am sure just about everyone can recall a time they were touched by or drawn to something that was not part of their familiar existence.

Dr. Robert Stoller, a California psychoanalyst interviewed people who practiced sadomasochism and found that they all had serious physical illness as children along with undergoing severe and terrifying pain due to hospitalization and painful medical treatments. Stoller writes (p. 125)[31] "As children, they consciously took their pain, their inexpressible rage, and reworked it in daydreams, in altered mental states, or in masturbation fantasies, so they could replay the story of the trauma with a happy ending and say to themselves; This time, I win."

In 1923 researcher Karl Lashley (p. 55)[32] in an attempt to map the brain "exposed a monkey's motor cortex, stimulated it in a particular place and observed the resulting movement". He then sewed the monkeys head back together and after a lapse in time repeated his experiment expecting to find the same movement in the particular parts of the monkey's body. To his surprise, he found that the movement related to the same stimulated areas in the brain cortex had changed, verifying that the brain is essentially a dynamic force and not fixed.

The mind as the perceiver, observer, and reflector of all things is by nature dynamic and fluid.

Traditional medicine and psychology will reject my thesis, but not on the basis of its merit, but merely because it does not produce the economic outcome that has been delivered by the current medical model as the healthcare system is the largest industry in the United States.

Dr. Benjamin Ross writes in his book Forbidden Cures; "You see, this powerful multibillion dollar industry (health care) controls all medical information. They effectively shut down all dissents". I know this to be a fact as I was invited to a meeting by a doctor friend of mine that in addition to traditional practices uses alternative therapies in his medical practice. At this meeting were over twenty medical

---

[31]   Doidge, Norman. The Brain That Changes Itself. 2007: Penguin Books, New York, New York.

[32]   Doidge, Norman. The Brain That Changes Itself. 2007: Penguin Books, New York, New York.

doctors who were being threatened with losing their licenses due to incorporating alternative treatments such a kelation therapy and naturopathic medicine. Not one doctor had been sued by a patient or had any complaints filed against them, but the "health police" working for the FDA wanted to discourage the use of natural substances such as herbs and vitamins as treatments. Using the laboratory produced analogs keep the profits for pharmaceutical companies rolling in.

Dr. Pert explains; (p. 253)[33] "since the natural substances are not patentable, there is no incentive for drug companies to study their benefits, and so the vast majority of M.D.'s who get their information about drugs from the drug companies, don't even know about them".

As I propose to explore the idea of cellular memory empowering the traumatized victim and bringing into consciousness and understanding those things that have fragmented the mind, I am also acutely aware of the dominance of pharmaceuticals in the mental health arenas that are used to treat trauma. In some cases, the drugs actually suppress the healing of trauma as they reduce the ability of the individual to understand the nuances of the causes and symptoms of their traumatic event as well as allow for the release of the person from the victimization of trauma.

While working in Chicago at a mental health clinic, I was assigned a client who would become catatonic over periods of time and spoke very little. She was constantly on medication and would be hospitalized periodically where she would receive even more medication along with electric shock treatments.

Working with her was very difficult mainly due to the fact she had little memory of her life and was not interested in talking. We decided to try some hypnosis and when she regressed to the age of six, she terrifyingly recalled how her father in a fit of jealous rage came into the

---

[33] Pert, Candace. Ph.D..Molecules of Emotion. 1997. Scribner: New York, New York

bedroom where she was sleeping in bed with her mother and stabbed her mother multiple times until she died. The little girl splattered with her mother's blood, had watched helplessly in horror believing she would be her father's next victim. To further terrorize the young girl, she was placed in the custody of her father after he got out of jail serving only a couple of years.

The client's recollection of the incident and helping her regain her empowerment brought the woman to a state of normalcy. The catatonic phases were gone and she became very talkative and animated during her following therapy sessions. The woman also started developing friendships and even became self-sustaining financially.

In today's pharmacological atmosphere, one suffering from depression is much more likely to be given a prescription for an antidepressant than a referral to a therapist.

To understand psychology as well as the psychology of trauma we are challenged by quantum physics to suspend our belief in what we perceive to be the reality of our world of matter and existence. The character of the rational mind is to find solutions to problems and categorize experiences. We are however, also intuitive, creative, inspired, and spiritual in nature.

Dr. Irving Ayle tells a story to illustrate the quagmire of relying on rational mind to explain our experience. He tells the story of an African God named Edsu. "In order to teach the inhabitants about reality he would appear in human form wearing a hat which was black on one side and white on the other." Edsu would walk through the village looking straight ahead, speaking to no one. Heated arguments, some even leading to bloodshed would develop between those people who stood on the left and those who stood on the right side of the human form of the God because if you stood on one side you would see the stranger in the white hat and if you stood on the other side you saw the stranger in the black hat.

Your Reality is clearly dependent on your viewpoint!

Regression Therapy and Methodology

Sometimes we choose our profession and sometimes it chooses us. I grew up in a traditional Christian Church and while I questioned many of the hypocrisies and dogmas I found in the church, Presbyterian Christianity formed my ideology about God. I had never even considered the idea of reincarnation.

In my early teens and twenties, I left all things of my dysfunctional past and like many people from my generation, I became consumed with materialism, family duties and in quiet parts of long sleepless nights, with the meaning of life.

My mother was diagnosed with terminal cancer when I was twenty-six and I became her caretaker for a year and a half until two weeks before her death when she was moved to Hospice where she could receive much needed morphine. Her death was the beginning of a turning point for me and my ideas about spirituality as well as reality itself.

Months after my mother's death I fell into a deep depression as the concept of living an unfulfilled life that ended by becoming a pile of ashes in a crematorium fire filled me with dread.

My mother was diagnosed in her twenties as being manic-depressive and struggled through most of her life with the illness. I suspect my father had the same diagnosis. My mother lead a quiet and sometimes loud life of desperation. I was trained at an early age in co-dependency which meant to go along to get along in simplest terms.

It became a habit for me to relinquish my needs or desires to please others, although I did have my bouts of rebellion. My marriage existed within this construct as I gave up the things that I loved such as school, art and music to please my husband. I found I had lost myself in this soulless existence. My life was continuing to be shaped by the dysfunctional destructive patterns of my parents ingrained in the information molecules of my medial temporal lobe which started as an unconscious process in infancy. I was lost in an abyss of faulty programing perpetuated by my own self-betrayal.

In addition, the minister at the church my mother attended regularly and gave her ten percent tithes that she could not afford to give, found he was too busy to be a comfort to her when she most needed him. It was actually the selfless nuns who still wore penguin habits that offered my mother solace. Religion became a bitter pill that I could no longer swallow. The sweet sappiness of living a loving Christian life vaporized like the innocent dreams of my traumatized childhood.

As I lay sleeping in bed one night which seems so very long ago, I was awakened from my deep forbidding sleep. There hovering at the foot of my bed was a large seven to eight-foot glowing luminous presence. It had human features somewhat, but not completely distinguishable and it raised me out of my bed, hovering as I could look down and see my husband lying in the bed. I was told many things about my life and my life to come and that I must leave my husband. I was frozen in fear and disbelief until I heard my mother speaking in a soothing voice "it's all right, I am here too". As I looked to the left, there was my mother standing next to my bed looking a bit translucent, but younger again and healthy.

I left my husband after he demanded I give up art, not so much for the art, but for the survival of my spirit. I knew then that there were mysteries beyond my comprehension and beyond time and space. For many years I was still bewildered by what had visited me that epochal night and now I believe that it was my higher self that came to empower me and free me from my bondage.

My next experience with unexplained phenomena illuminated the character of a universal mind, although I must admit that I have not even scratched the surface of knowledge.

While hiking through a canyon in Sedona with my second husband, we rested at the top of a crest overlooking the beautiful landscape of the canyon pass. As we sat there enjoying the majestic view, we both noticed a large wavy mass much like looking at an energy ball that had the colors and movement of an oil slick, moving through the canyon bending the tree tops as it passed over them. It continued to move toward us as we watched in awe and amazement and then it came to hover in front of me. Without warning it moved into my body and started downloading information about spiritual nature at an incredibly rapid pace. My husband said later that he tried to move toward me and yet was kept away as if by an invisible barrier. I felt an incredible exhilaration as the energy overtook me and then I began to realize my body was too frail to contain the massive energy and just when I thought I would die, the mass leapt from my body and traveled back from where it had come.

My spiritual path was defined at that moment, although the journey had just begun. I returned home to Virginia and the following day I received a call from a person I did not know telling me to come and study with a teacher that I had never heard of. The class was regression therapy and I was not sure what I was getting into.

Over the next two years I studied hypnotherapy, regression therapy, and Neuro Linguistic Programming (NLP). I have been a practicing regression therapist for the past twenty years. During that time, I also attended school for Psychology, Gestalt Therapy, art therapy, counseling, and theology in order that I develop a well-rounded therapeutic approach so I could be better equipped to help facilitate others in their healing process.

Through the years, I have worked in a psychiatric hospital, mental health center, residential treatment, addictions detox center, contract therapist to schools, private practice and as a crisis therapist. I have seen what works and what does not work, and in truth, most therapeutic styles have strong points and success stories. Regression therapy is not the "way", but is proposed as another approach which may offer positive results and relief from the effects of trauma for individuals. Regression therapy is one of the more efficient therapies as far as time effectiveness and providing lasting relief from the effects of trauma, however, it can also be dangerous if facilitated by an untrained person.

The facilitator can trigger the traumatized cellular memories from the past and not complete the process of moving the person beyond the trauma allowing for transmutation of the negative energy in addition to not completing the final steps of healing and empowerment. The individual is left with a sense of being re-traumatized and may become emotionally destabilized for a period of time.

The methodology used in regression therapy is much like the hypnotist uses or a Gestalt experiment. It begins with putting the subject in a deep state of relaxation. Many hypnotists work in an alpha state. I like to move the client deeper down into a theta state through a process of relaxation and guided imagery. It is important that they are deeply hypnotized so that the client finds his/her hidden memories more accessible. It is very important to never give directives to the hypnotized subject as they are in a highly suggestive state. I would not direct a person under hypnosis to go to a past life in Egypt for example. In some ways the unconscious mind is like a sponge and will absorb the information it is fed. I have on rare occasions asked a client to go to the past life that caused the problems they are having when they continually get stuck in telling a story over and over from present life.

Hypnotic suggestion does have its place when it is used with a client to stop smoking, lose weight, control pain, develop good study habits, and so on.

Sidney Rosen wrote a book titled "My Voice Will Go With You" about Milton H. Erickson who was a genius in the field of Hypnotherapy. He states in his book:[34](p.26)

"Trance, according to Erickson, is the state in which learning and openness to change are most likely to occur. It does not refer to an induced somnolent state. Patients are not "put under" by the therapist, nor are they out of control and directed by the will of another person. Trance, in fact, is a natural state experienced by everyone. Our most familiar experience takes place when we daydream, but other trance states can occur when we meditate, pray, or perform exercises – such as jogging, which has sometimes been called "meditation in motion."

In a trance state, individuals are often more intuitively connected to answers about the meaning of symbols, dreams, and situations that they are dealing with in their lives. It is as if once the conscious mind along with its critical values is reduced, the unconscious is able to tap into a level of higher awareness. The therapist in a sense, facilitates the client into focusing their attention inwards toward the unconscious response mechanism thereby bringing the unconscious information into awareness.

Gil Boyne, a well known hypnotherapist and past teacher of mine

---

[34]   Rosen, Sidney, My Voice Will Go With You. 1982, W.W. Norton, New York, New York

stated:[35] "The true ministry of the hypnotherapist is to heal the self-induced blindness that has created a cloud of unknowing".

Boyne also wrote about the benefits of the process of hypnosis with what he termed "Phenomena of Trance". He identified six strategies for psychological healing which may occur through the hypnotic process with much more speed and efficiency than some traditional psychotherapies. They are as follows:

1. The development and expression of deductive processing of though and imagery.

2. The ability to stimulate memory recall and simultaneously revive attached feeling content.

3. An enhanced capacity to quickly develop an emotionalized relationship (rapport) with the helping person.

4. A tremendously heightened capacity to internalize new and different ideas (programming) presented by the helper, utilizing a variety of methods such as implication, supposition, and the use of multiple level communication.

5. Heightened potential for stimulation and manipulation of subconscious memories, scripts, belief systems, and emotionalized attitudes which form the basis for the client's counterproductive behavior.

6. Accessibility to levels of irrational, deductive processing, which generate inhibition and feelings of helplessness expressed in specific forms of maladaptive behavior.

7. Accessibility to levels of irrational, deductive processing, which generate inhibition and feelings of helplessness expressed in specific forms of maladaptive behavior.

---

[35] Boyne, Gil. Transforming Therapy, A New Approach to Hypnotherapy. Westwood Publishing, Glendale, Caifornia

Basically, with regard to healing trauma, hypnosis allows the individual to restructure a traumatic event that has taken place within the element of their cellular memory reaction. The goal is for an experience to occur which will re-inform and transform the client by "affecting the very root of their subconscious experience", so stated by Calvin Banyan[36] who wrote an advanced teaching guide for hypnotherapists.

Banyan also recommends that the hypnotherapist "maintain a leadership role at the start of the session. My teacher, Dr. Long also said "be the strong supportive mother archetype". They also taught to ask if the client was ready to be hypnotized and prepared for the process. It is important that the client does not feel coerced, but has a willing attitude.

Prior to hypnosis, I always spend time answering questions, explaining the experience of hypnosis and letting the client know that they are in charge of the process so they do not feel they might be out of control or made to do something against their will.

When hypnotizing a client, the therapist must be aware of subtle changes that are occurring within the subject. Erickson terms it "response attentiveness". The individual will become almost completely immobile, their breathing will be shallow, there will be a flattening of their facial expressions and sometimes a tearing in the corners of their eye. I always ask that clients close their eyes, however, some hypnotherapists work with eyes open having the individual stare at a particular spot. One of the most prominent indicators for me that a person is hypnotized it that a wall of energy comes out about a foot from the body. This energy field lets me know that the person has succumbed to the hypnotic process and are in a deep state of relaxation.

---

36   Banyan, Calvin. Hypnosis and Hypnotherapy. 2001: Abbot Publishing House, Minnesota.

Interesting components of the hypnotized subject is that they are literal in their processing of the therapist questioning and that they are not able to answer "why" questions which requires a conscious deduction. Without the conscious mind to interject projections, criticisms, and judgments, the unconscious mind seems more involved in actual events than assumptions.

During my training, my teacher taught us not to ask "why" questions, although on occasion in the early stages of my regression work a "why" question would slip out unconsciously such as "Why did you do that?". I would find the client would not be able to answer the question. The rules of questioning the client were basically to stay with "where, what, when" and "how".

Erickson believed the tales told by his clients were archetypal patterns much like fairy tales or folk mythology. I believe the stories to be much more related to the truth, however, it does not matter if they are archetypal or actual as long as they bring lasting relief to the client. We are actually dealing with the blocked cellular energy connected to trauma much more than the story. By changing the story to a more positive and compassionate script which empowers the client instead of leaving them with a sense of helplessness, we are able to complete the feedback loop building a sense of personal dominion and control over one's life. This new found control helps people build a new sense of confidence which develops a greater feeling of self-worth.

During the trance state as the story of trauma evolves, the subject will actually begin to have heightened awareness of sensory perceptions. They are acutely aware of their feelings, sights, sounds, smells and environment. Often they become frightened, tearful, and reluctant to proceed with the process. Yet this is precisely the point that the therapist must push through the blocks in order to bring a resolve to the incident of the trauma.

There are four stages of brain wave activity and each condition is linked to a different state of consciousness facilitating the brain to provide different tasks. The stages are the Alpha state seen in wakefulness, and yet a relaxed and effortless alertness such as when one is watching TV or listening to music. The Beta state which oscillates at a faster rate and is present in stressful situations or where there is more mental focus such as taking a test in school. Theta brain waves are produced in light sleep and drowsiness such as rim sleep which is the dreaming state and delta brain waves are the slowest oscillating representing deep sleep.

It is important in my process for regression therapy to bring the client to a state of theta waves. The client generally starts in the alpha state, but I continue throughout the process of hypnosis to continue to take the client to a lower oscillating brain wave in order to facilitate a richer and more vivid experience with the unconscious mind.

Hypnosis starts with a general visualization of a stairway and counting down while the client descends the stairs into a more relaxed state. I then proceed to take the client on a visual journey through guided imagery which provides them with an enjoyable experience leading then to become even more relaxed. The next step is to engage them with feelings asking the client "How do you feel" and "where in your body do you feel that feeling?". I often joke with client's that I am boring them to the point that the conscious mind shuts down, but actually there is a lot of truth in that approach.

It is also important to clarify the event with the client or restate back to the client the statements they have made thereby anchoring the experience in their mind. Often when a client is having difficulty visualizing an experience I ask them for additional nonthreatening details such as whether they are indoors or out, what is the weather like, what is the furniture like, describe your clothing, hair, what you are wearing on your feet. Non-threatening questions help the client to relax and allow the scene to unfold. I will then proceed by asking them to become more aware if there are other people around them, what is happening, and how they are feeling.

Once the client has discovered the origins of the trauma, expressed the feelings related to the trauma, released the traumatic energy and gained a greater understanding of the situation, it is also important for the client to experience a feeling of empowerment and spiritual alignment to a cosmic consciousness that supports their enrichment and self-awareness. Once one accepts their experiences as a process of karma, growing and self-actualization, life's tribulations take on a different meaning. One moves from the role of victim to a player in the cosmic dance of life. This does not mean that one necessarily views trauma with detachment or is unaffected by negative experiences, it just means that the unconscious residue of trauma does not continually derail their life's positive progression.

Transcripts from Past Life Regressions

My first volunteer for my regression research will be called John as his real name is kept confidential. John is a Native American/Hispanic man in his fifties and he was the victim of mental/physical/and sexual abuse as a child. John served in Viet Nam as a young man where he learned Chinese and became a translator intercepting messages from the enemy. After the military he married and settled into a corporate job.

John volunteered to participate in my research due to the fact he was going through severe depression after the breakup of his twenty-five-year marriage to an abusive woman. On one level he knew that dissolving the marriage would have its benefits as he would be free of the criticisms of his wife and yet he felt conflicting feelings of failure and also the financial loses that go along with divorce.

John's session was audio taped and the following transcript was derived from the tapes. Some parts were inaudible and so noted in the transcript. The actual hypnosis induction was left out of the tape recording and transcript do to the element of time as I can easily spend a half hour in the process of hypnotizing the subject to a deep level.

John's First Session

Therapist: "Open the box and look inside, tell me what you see in the box."

John: "I don't know."

Therapist: "Look inside the box."

John: "I smell cedar. It's my lungs. It hurts my lungs."

Therapist: "What makes it hurt your lungs? Go into that energy. What color would that energy be."

John: Red. "Crimson red."

Therapist:" Go into that red energy. I am going to take you to the first place you remember feeling that same energy. One, two, three – go back to that first place you remember feeling the same pain in your lungs."

John: "I'm indoors."

Therapist: "Describe the indoors."

John: "Let me look."

Therapist: "Look around. Is there furniture in there?"

John: "Very little…rustic. The room is a cabin like…the smell of cedar is overwhelming."

Therapist: "Are you alone or are there others with you?"

John: "I feel a presence, but I am not seeing anyone. My arms hurt. Oh God, they hurt."

Therapist: "What's hurting your arms?"

John: "Like I'm bound."

Therapist: "Look down at your feet, describe what you are wearing on your feet."

John: "Nothing."

Therapist: "Look at your hands, are they big or small."

John: "There real small."

Therapist: "Look at your hair – is it long or short?"

John: "About medium."

Therapist: "What color is your hair?"

John: "Brown"

Therapist: "Look at your face, are you male or female?"

John: "male"

Therapist: "What clothing are you wearing?"

John: "Strange…um…kind of like long loose pants, not like regular pants and a torn shirt."

Therapist:" Look at your face, describe your face to me."

John: "I would say Caucasian."

Therapist: "What is happening there? He is bound in the cabin. What is happening?"

John: "He is not sure what's going to happen. It's almost like he's been jailed. I don't know."

Therapist:" I am going to take you back to mealtime. I am going to count to three, two, one and go back to mealtime. Is he indoors or outdoors?"

John: "Indoors"

Therapist: "Describe the indoors."

John: "Light and airy…Lots of open windows."

Therapist: "Look around at the furniture."

John: "It looks rich."

Therapist: "Describe the meal table."

John: "Long, very long, probably eight to twelve chairs."

Therapist: "Look around the table and tell me what other people are there."

John: "Mom and dad, two other kids."

Therapist: "How does he feel there in the family? How does he feel at mealtime there?"

John: "Like he is out of place. Unwanted."

Therapist: "I want you to listen for his name. Have someone in the room call him by his name. What name do they call him by?"

John: "George"

Therapist: "About how old is George?"

John: "About six or seven."

Therapist: "Where is he feeling that unwanted feeling in his body?"

John: "In his chest."

Therapist: "What color is that energy there in his chest?"

John: "Yellow white."

Therapist: "I am going to take you to the next main event in George's life. I am going to count you there three, two, one, is he indoors or out?"

John: "Outdoors"

Therapist: "Describe the outdoors."

John: "Tall trees, a forest. I'm lost."

Therapist: "How did you come to be in the forest?"

John: "I was told to wait there."

Therapist: "Who told you to wait there?"

John: "Father, I believe."

Therapist: "How old is George?"

John: "About three or four. He is feeling scared."

Therapist: "Where is he feeling that scared feeling in his body."

John: "In the pit of his stomach."

Therapist: "What color is that energy there in the pit of his stomach?"

John: "Yellow green"

Therapist: "What happens? What does his father do?"

John: "He tells him stay there. I'm coming back."

Therapist: "Does he come back?"

John: "Yes eventually......Oh, the pain in my shoulder!"

Therapist: "What's happening there?"

John: "He's pulling my arm."

Therapist: "The father?"

John: "Yes, my father."

Therapist: "Now I am going to take you to the next main event, counting three, two, one, is George indoors or out."

John: Indoors. "Deep breathing. Painful sounds. First breath."

Therapist: "Is George being born?"

John: "I think so."

Therapist: "What's happening, how is he feeling?"

John: "He feels unwelcome."

Therapist: "Where in his body does he feel unwelcome?"

John: "In his neck and shoulders."

Therapist: "Feel the energy – if that were a color what would it be?"

John: "Reddish orange"

Therapist: "Move into that energy in the shoulders and the neck. I am going to count you back to the first time you felt that reddish orange energy in the neck and shoulders. Three, two, one, go back to the first time. Are you indoors or out?"

John: "Outdoors."

Therapist: "Describe the outdoors."

John: "Open meadow. Large fire with many people." AT THIS POINT JOHN HAS JUMPED INTO ANOTHER LIFE TIME. I DECIDED TO SEE WHERE HE IS GOING RATHER THAN TAKE HIM BACK TO THE LIFETIME OF GEORGE. IT IS IMPORTANT TO HONOR THE SOUL'S JOURNEY AS IT

GENERALLY KNOWS WHERE TO GO TO ADDRESS THE MOST IMPORANT ISSUES FOR HEALING.

Therapist: "Look at your feet. What are you wearing on your feet?"

John: "Moccasins."

Therapist: "What clothing are you wearing?"

John: "Loin cloth"

Therapist: "Look at your hair, is it long or short."

John: "Long"

Therapist: "What color is your hair?"

John: "Black"

Therapist: "Look around at the people you are with. What race are these people?"

THERAPIST CAN'T UNDERSTAND CLIENTS ANSWER

Therapist: "How do you feel with these people?"

John: "Good"

Therapist: "Where do you feel that good feeling in your body?"

John: "In my heart, but I still have the pain in my shoulder."

Therapist: "Tell me what is happening there?"

John: "It's like a gathering."

Therapist: "have someone there call you by your name. Listen for your name."

John: "Free Spirit."

Therapist: "I am going to take you to the net main event in Free Spirit's life. Counting three, two, one, are you indoors or out?"

John: "Outdoors"

Therapist: "Describe what is happening."

John: "Pain! Pain in my shoulder!" CLIENT APPEARS TO BE IN PAIN AND STARTS RUBBING HIS SHOULDER.

Therapist: "What's happening?"

John: "I've been wounded or injured."

Therapist: "Look around and tell me what's happening."

John: "Oh my God! Oh God!" CLIENT IS YELLING OUT.

Therapist: "Separate from the pain, stay with the energy. Tell me what's happening."

John: "I've been attacked."

Therapist: "And who attacked you?"

John: "Oh God! A bear!" CLIENT IS VISIBLY IN PAIN.

Therapist: "Separate from the pain, tell me what happened."

John: "He hit me in the shoulder. He knocked me to the ground. I laid perfectly still. I tried not to move. I was afraid he would come back."

Therapist: "Did he leave?"

John: "He just left."

Therapist: "I am counting you to the next main event in Free Spirit's life, counting three, two, one, is he indoors or out."

John: Indoors. "In a large Teepee. Preparing."

Therapist: "What is he preparing for?"

John: "Spirit Quest"

Therapist: "How is he feeling about that?"

John: "Very excited."

Therapist: "Are there others there with him or is he alone?"

John: "He is alone. They are sending me to the forest to a predetermined place.

Therapist: Tell me what happens."

John: "I sit and make a small fire opening up." I AM GUESSING OPENING SPIRITUALLY.

Therapist: "How does it feel sitting there opening up?"

John: "That's when the bear comes."

Therapist: "I want Free Spirit to go there right before his death. Is Free Spirit indoors or out?"

John: "Out"

Therapist: "Describe what's happening."

John: "He's alone, very alone."

Therapist: "Look at his face. Is he young or old?"

John: "Very old. He has lived a long life."

Therapist: "How is he feeling there before his death?"

John: "Very calm, satisfied."

Therapist: "Is he happy there."

John: "He is happy, but he is sad that it is so short."

Therapist:" I am going to count you back to the time Free Spirit is a young man on a vision quest. Three, two, one, go right back there, plant your feet firmly there. You are on a vision quest and the bear comes. Tell me what happens."

John: "I stand there facing him and he rears up and hits me in the right shoulder. He pushes me to the ground and stands over my back and I don't move. I am terrified to move, fearful, frightened, and then he walks off."

Therapist: "How does Free Spirit feel now?"

John: "Calm, still frightened, but I lay still and I can hear him moving away."

Therapist: "Then what happens to the bear. Speak to the bear on this vision quest."

John: "His soul soars above me and takes away all the pain."

Therapist: "What happens when Free Spirit returns to the village?"

John: "I don't understand. They cheer; they think I am very strong. They see me as being stronger than I am."

Therapist: "Be there with the people. Listen for the name of the tribe."

John: "Okeechobee" THERE IS EVIDENCE A LARGE NATIVE POPULATION SETTLED FOUR THOUSAND YEARS AGO AT LAKE OKEECHOBEE WHICH IS A SEMINOLE WORD FOR "BIG WATER". THERE ARE STILL REMNANTS OF THE SEMINOLE NATION THAT EXISTS CURRENTLY IN THE

OKEECHOBEE AREA. JOHN LIVES IN NEW MEXICO AND HAD NO KNOWLEDGE OF A PLACE IN FLORIDA CALLED OKEECHOBEE.

Therapist: "Does Free Spirit learn how to fight? Do they teach him how to fight?"

John: "yes."

Therapist: "I am going to count you to the time when Free Spirit was sent to fight as a warrior. I am going to count you to battle, three, two, one."

John: "Were being attacked. It is as if I have an aura around me."

Therapist: "Who is attacking?"

John: "Another tribe. It's almost like they are afraid to attack me. Like they are just ghosts when they get real close."

Therapist: "How does it feel there in battle?"

John: "That he brings death, it brings sorrow to his heart."

Therapist: "I am going to count Free Spirit to the next main event, three, two, one – go there to the next event is he indoors or outdoors?"

John: "Outdoors."

Therapist: "Describe what's happening."

John: "He just came upon a settlement -White people."

Therapist: "What happened?"

John: "We murdered all the men. I take a white, red headed woman."

Therapist: "How does she feel?"

John: "Scared, Terrified."

Therapist: "What about the children?"

John: "They rot."

Therapist: "What happens when you take the women back to the camp?"

John: "There's four of them. Everybody takes one." I ASSUME HE MEANS THE MEN WHO RAID THE SETTEMENT.

Therapist: "How do the women feel?"

John: "Really scared."

Therapist: "Feel her energy how does she feel?"

John: "Fear, anger, anguish."

Therapist: "Have you ever felt that same energy in this lifetime?"

John: "No, not in this lifetime."

Therapist: "Tell me what is making you feel sad?" CLIENT IS CRYING

John: "She won't love me."

Therapist: "Does Free Spirit love this woman he took?"

John: "Immensely"

Therapist: "Did she ever love him?"

John: "No."

Therapist: "Did he ever return her?"

John: "No."

Therapist: "How did he actually feel about taking her."

John: "He felt good, but he couldn't make her love him." CLIENT IS VERY EMOTIONAL

Therapist: "What happened to the woman?"

John: "She died."

Therapist: "What caused her death?"

John: "Heartbreak."

Therapist: "How did Free Spirit feel about that?"

John: "He should have returned her." CLIENT IS VERY TEARFUL.

Therapist: "I am going to take you right now to right before Free Spirit dies, taking you to the time and place right before he dies. Tell me what is Free Spirit dying from?"

John: "I'm not sure. He's an old man. Well he is old, but he is not as old as he should have been. It was a premature death and he feels that it is because of what he has done, the damage that he caused, even though his heart was filled with love. The anger and the hate was all that he showed."

Therapist: "Let him go ahead and die and let me know when he can look down on his body."

John: "Now."

Therapist: "How is he feeling?"

John: "Free"

Therapist: "Good, how else is he feeling?"

John: "He wishes he could go back and change things."

Therapist: "Have him look back over that life time and tell me what lesson could he learn in that life?"

John: "That love can't be forced."

Therapist: "Now, I am going to count you to the very next lifetime. One, Two, Three are you indoors or out?"

John: "Outdoors."

Therapist: "Describe where you are."

John: "On the icy shores."

Therapist: "Look down at your feet. What are you wearing on your feet?"

John: "Tall fur boots."

Therapist: "What are you wearing?"

John: "Furs."

Therapist: "Look at your face."

John: "It's weathered from the cold."

Therapist: "What's happening there by the ice."

John: "I'm preparing."

Therapist: "What are you preparing?"

John: "I'm going home."

Therapist: "How are you feeling?"

John: "Exuberant."

Therapist: "Look around and have someone call you by your name. What name do they call you by?"

John: "I don't know; I am at an Eskimo village."

Therapist: "How do you feel there in the village?"

John: "Proud – he's like a leader."

Therapist: "Does he have a family?"

John: "Yes"

Therapist: "I am going to count you down to a mealtime with the family. Place your feet firmly there – are you indoors or out?"

John: "Indoors."

Therapist: "Describe the indoors."

John: "I'm a seal hunter. Inuit, white everywhere."

Therapist: "What are you eating?"

John: "I believe were eating seal."

Therapist: "How are you feeling?"

John: "Good."

Therapist: "Tell me about his children."

John: "A young boy and a young girl. Happy."

Therapist: "Feel the energy of those children; have you felt that energy before?"

John: "Not sure."

Therapist: "How about his wife how does he feel about his wife?"

John: "He loves her and she loves him."

THE NEXT PART OF THE TAPE WAS INAUDIBLE, HOWEVER THE CLIENT GOES ON TO DESCRIBE GOING ON A WHALE HUNTING TRIP AND GETTING HIS FOOT CAUGHT IN ONE OF THE THICK ROPE FISHING LINES AND BEING PULLED OVERBOARD. HE RECALLS AS HE GOES INTO THE WATER LOOKING DIRECTLY INTO THE WHALES EYE AND FEELING AS IF HE MADE CONTACT WITH THE WHALE. THE CLIENT DIED DROWNING IN

THE FREEZING WATER. THE INCIDENT WAS RETOLD TO ME THROUGH RECOLLECTION BY THE CLIENT.

THE IMPORTANCE OF THE STORY OF GEORGE IN THE BEGINNING OF THE REGRESSION WAS TO UNDERSTAND THROUGH KARMA WHAT IT WOULD FEEL LIKE LIVING IN A FAMILY WHERE YOU FELT YOU DID NOT BELONG. IN THIS WAY THE CLIENT WAS ABLE TO EXPERIENCE THE DIFFICULTY OF THE WHITE WOMAN HE CAPTURED WHEN HE WAS NATIVE AMERICAN.

THE CLIENT IS NOW READY TO DEAL WITH HIS TRAUMA FROM THIS LIFE AS HE TRUSTS IN THE PROCESS SO I DECIDE TO TAKE HIM TO HIS CURRENT LIFE AS THE CLIENT SUFFERED MANY TRAUMAS AND NEEDED TO BRING THEM TO CONSCIOUS AWARENESS SO THAT HE COULD REGAIN HIS PERSONAL POWER AND RELEASE NEGATIVE PATTERNS THAT HE HAD WITH HIS RECENTLY SEPARATED WIFE.

Therapist: "I am going to take you home now. Three, two, one, look around and describe your home to me."

John: "Stucco walls, wood floor."

Therapist: "How do your parents feel about you?"

John: "Excited."

Therapist: "Tell me what year this is?"

John: "I don't know…1956…it's warm."

Therapist: "This is your parents. Look at your dad again. What race is your dad?"

John: "He was born Indian."

Therapist: "How does he feel about you?"

John: "Excited, but strange my parents argue."

Therapist: "What do they argue about?"

John: "His dad."

Therapist: "What makes them argue about his dad?"

John: CLIENT IS SOBBING... "That I am not his son. He thinks I'm his fathers."

Therapist: "What does your mother say?"

John: "She is fighting with him about it."

Therapist: "What happens?"

John: "My grandfather comes."

Therapist: "What happens?"

John: "A fight and argument and then he leaves."

Therapist: "What does your grandfather say when your father accuses him of being the father."

John: "He denies it....Ooo...Ooo jeez...." CLIENT CRYING

Therapist: "What's happening? Going to the next main event."

John: "The police are there."

Therapist: "What caused the police to come?"

John: "My grandfather is dead."

Therapist: "What caused him to die?"

John: "He was beat up and had a heart attack."

Therapist: "Bring up that energy. How did you feel about your grandfather?"

John: "I didn't know him."

Therapist: "What caused them to beat him up?"

John: "They wanted money."

Therapist: "Go to the next main event, counting three, two, one... go there to the next main event and are you indoors or outdoors."

John: "Indoors. I'm in my bedroom. No! No!" CLIENT IS CRYING. CLIENT IS BEING ABUSED, BUT IS EMBARRASED TO SAY IT.

Therapist: "who is doing it?"

John: "Mom"

Therapist: "Go into her energy. What is going on? How does she feel?" IF THE CLIENT FEELS UNCOMFORTABLE TELLING WHAT IS HAPPENING, IT IS NOT IMPORTANT THAT THE THERAPIST KNOWS AS LONG AS THE CLIENT KNOWS. IT DOES HELP THE CLIENT TO UNDERSTAND WHAT IS MOTIVATING THEIR PERPETRATOR SO THE CLIENT DOES NOT FEEL ANY RESPONSIBILITY ABOUT WHAT IS HAPPENING. THE CLIENTS MOTHER HAD BEEN SEXUALLY ABUSED FOR YEARS AS A CHILD AND UNCONCIOUSLY REENACTS HER SEXUAL ABUSE WITH MALES. CLIENT CARRIED A LOT OF GUILT AND SHAME WHICH HE WAS ABLE TO RELEASE REALIZING IT WAS NOT HIS FAULT AS HE WAS A CHILD.

John: "No! She thinks what she is doing is right. I don't know." CLIENT APPEARS TO BE IN PAIN.

Therapist: "Separate the pain. Imagine a white light coming like the white light at death. Imagine a white light of God coming to protect you, to heal you. Open every cell and poor of your body and let the white light stream down and fill your body so you will be one with the creator energy the light will come down through your face, your shoulders, all that energy from being injured by the bear, pulled as a child, pulled into the water, see all the dark energy and it is being pushed out of the body. All the negative things of the past no longer serve you and you are releasing them. You have an awareness of the life cycle and the light moves down your shoulders, arms, chest, especially areas where you had cancer. All the negative cellular energy is leaving your body now and every part of your body is healing now. You are returning to perfection. You are releasing all guilt – all the guilt that has plagued you from trying to force your will, regrets and sorrows can now be released, all those bad feelings are released so that you will have only happiness and the light filling your body.

The light will now form a mist and the mist will form a beautiful golden egg, impenetrable. You can imagine someone trying to pierce the egg but they cannot. You are pure love, you are loved, you are cared for, you are protected, you are one with the creator energy. Now go back there and get the man before he goes into the water and pull him into the egg and tell him he is safe and loved. Tel him how you admire his love and his courage as he did a good job of loving his family. Now go back to Free Spirit and let me know when he is in the egg by saying now out loud."

John: "Now."

Therapist: "Good. Now pull him into the egg and tell him he is forgiven, that you love and honor him. Tell him how your honor his courage and strength. He was willful and you are aware of that, but you forgive him and release him. Now go back to George and tell him you are grateful to him as he taught you what it was like to live somewhere where he felt he did not belong. When you come back you will be wide awake, aware, and live happily each and every day becoming healthier, happier, creating your life in a way that will be of the highest benefit to you."

CLIENT IS BROUGHT BACK TO THE PRESENT AND OUT OF HIS STATE OF HYPNOSIS.

John is a bit shaken by his regression and asks if this was true. I can only offer evidence of the emotions that were attached to his past life experiences, but the most important will be the life changes that occur in his life. John reports that he actually felt the experiences as they were happening as well as the fear, joy, sadness, and love.

When John was asked to report on his experience a few months later to give time for the effects of the regression to become more concrete, John sent this answer:

"We are all a culmination of all that was. Understanding gained through Past Life Regression has given me the tools to take the information and realize what mistakes I have made and use them to turn my life around. I can also see the pitfalls, look at them and make better choices in what is to follow. Having done this has made me a happier person and better equipped to maintain that happiness and deal with life's' challenges using a better understanding of myself."   John

Two years after John's regression he is doing quite well. He no longer suffers from depression or the guilt brought about by his early childhood experiences. He has forgiven his mother, although he has little contact with her. He has reconnected with many of his cousins and is enjoying the new found relationships. He found out about his mother's sexual abuse as a child as well as sexual abuse to other family members. John has also developed a new perspective on his father who was an alcoholic who killed himself and now sees all the wonderful positive qualities that his father had. His father was a wonderful artist, musician and carpenter which are qualities that John inherited. John has also reconnected with his Native American heritage which was forbidden to engage in by his mother as she felt ashamed of her own Native American heritage and claimed only her Hispanic roots. John's father was full Native American.

John now remembers the fun that he had with his father hunting and fishing as those memories had been repressed due to the trauma of his childhood. John also moved into a new home which he is really enjoying and has found a very positive relationship with a woman who is very supportive and caring.

Sarah's Regression

Sarah is an African American woman in her thirties who is married and has two children. Sarah does not believe in past lives, but does not disbelieve and is willing to try the regression. Sarah had a difficult life growing up as there were four siblings in a single parent home. Sarah's mother was loving and hardworking, but had difficulty raising her children with little income and emotional support.

I have shared cases with Sarah who works for Department of Children and Family Services and know her to be a truly kind, caring and hard working woman. She is also very intelligent and holds a master's degree in social work. While I know her level of competency through working with her, I had no knowledge of her personal life prior to the regression.

The session starts after several minutes of induction and client has been asked to locate a box in a large chamber.

Sarah: "There is a large wooden box with a lock on it."

Therapist: "Look at the wooden box with the lock on it. Use your light to help you see what is in the box."

Sarah: "A snake."

Therapist: "When you see the snake in the box is it big or small?"

Sarah: "Small"

Therapist: "How do you feel when you see the snake?"

Sarah: "I feel bad for it."

Therapist: "Pick it up and hold it in your hands, describe the snake for me."

Sarah: "Green and yellow."

Therapist: "How do you feel as your holding the snake there?"

Sarah: "It's wiggling around in my hand."

Therapist: "How does it make you feel, what feelings come to mind?"

Sarah: "Confusion."

Therapist: "Feel that confusion, where in your body do you most feel the confusion?

Sarah: "In my head and my belly."

Therapist: "I want you to go to that energy there in your head and your belly and I want you to tell me what energy would that be if it were a color?"

Sarah: "Red"

Therapist: "Go into that red energy there in your belly and if that red energy could speak what would it say?"

Sarah: "Who put you here?"

Therapist: "Go into that red energy and I'm going to count you back to the very first time and place that you remember feeling that same red confused energy in your body. One, two, three – are you indoors or out?"

Sarah: "Indoors – we lived in an old apartment when I was a kid."

Therapist: "Look at your clothes, what are you wearing?"

Sarah: "Shorts and a shirt."

Therapist: "Are there others with you?"

Sarah: "My brothers and sisters are there."

Therapist: "What's happening there with your brothers and sisters?"

Sarah: "Were sitting in the living room talking."

Therapist: "And then what happens?"

Sarah: "I don't feel like I am a part of them."

Therapist: "How did that feel?"

Sarah: "Sometimes it's sad."

Therapist: "Where do you feel that sadness in your body?"

Sarah: "In my belly."

Therapist: "Go there in your belly, into the sadness. What color would that energy be if it were a color. I want you to go to the very first time that you felt that same yellow energy and I am going to count you back there. One, two, three, are you indoors or out?"

Sarah: "Inside, at a store."

Therapist: "Look at your feet, what are you wearing on your feet?"

Sarah: "Tennis shoes"

Therapist: "How old are you?"

Sarah: "About five."

Therapist: "What's happening?"

Sarah: "I can't find my mom."

Therapist: "Are you feeling scared?"

Sarah: "Yes"

Therapist: "What's happening?"

Sarah: "I am running through the store. I went to find my sister, but she is gone. I found someone in the store to help me."

Therapist: "What happened next?"

Sarah: "They found her."

Therapist: "How did you feel back there when you felt lost and scared? Where did you feel the energy?"

Sarah: "More in my head."

Therapist: "Good. Go into that energy in your head that feeling of being scared, lost, and feel that energy there in your head and if the energy were a color what color would it be?"

Sarah: "Black"

Therapist: "Feel that black energy in your head. I want to take you back to the very first time you felt the energy there in your head. Go right back there and tell me what you see."

Sarah: "Nothing."

Therapist: "Release that black energy. Going back to the very first time you felt that energy. …(Large bang made by the therapist) Release the energy."

Sarah: "I'm indoors, the same apartment."

Therapist: "What's happening?"

Sarah: "Arguing, my mother and brother are arguing." (Client begins crying)

Therapist: "Bring that energy up. Bring up that emotion. What is happening next, what is making you feel sad?"

Sarah: (client is crying) "He's done some things. He's in trouble."

Therapist: "Go into the energy of your brother. What is he doing?"

Sarah: "He's yelling at my mom."

Therapist: "What makes him yell at your mom?"

Sarah: "He doesn't want to listen to her. He's in a bad crowd."

Therapist: "What's making you sad and scared?"

Sarah: "I don't like arguing."

Therapist: "Go into that feeling of arguing and tell me where do you feel that feeling most in your body?"

Sarah: "In my hands."

Therapist: "Feel that energy there in your hands. Move into that energy and what color would it be."

Sarah: "Green."

Therapist: "Go into that green energy and I am going to count you back to the first time you remember feeling that same green energy in your body. Counting back one, two, three, plant your feet firmly there, are you indoors or out?"

Sarah: "Indoors, I'm in a room that I share with my sister."

Therapist: "About how old are you?"

Sarah: "About the same age."

Therapist; "What's happening there?"

Sarah: "She's got a knife. She says she wants to kill herself."

Therapist: "How are you feeling?"

Sarah: "Scared."

Therapist: "Stay right there with the energy. Now I want you to go to a past life and go to the very first time you felt that same sadness and fear, the same energy that you are feeling now. I am going to count you back the very first time you felt that same scared energy. One, two, three, go right back there and tell me what are you wearing on your feet?"

Sarah: "I don't know if this is right."

Therapist: "Whatever images come to mind just say them."

Sarah: "Their not good shoes, their tattered shoes."

Therapist: "Are you indoors or out."

Sarah: "I'm indoors, but I'm looking out of the door."

Therapist: "What clothing are you wearing?"

Sarah: "Old clothing, servant style clothes."

Therapist: "Look at your hands, are they big or small?"

Sarah: "Big"

Therapist: "Look at your hair is it long or short?"

Sarah: "It's tied up."

Therapist: "Are you male or female?"

Sarah: "Female"

Therapist: "Tell me what you are doing there inside looking out. What's happening?

Sarah: "I'm standing in a little shack."

Therapist: "Are you alone or are there others with you."

Sarah: "I'm not sure."

Therapist: "I'm going to take you to a mealtime. Three, two, one, are you indoors or out?"

Sarah: "I'm not sure. I can't see. I don't know if it is dark outside. I see a fire. People are sitting."

Therapist: "Go look and see what the people are eating." I USE MEALTIME TO GROUND THE PERSON IN THE PAST LIFE EXPERIENCE AND MEMORY, AS IT IS A NON-THREATNING RECOLLECTION.

Sarah: "I don't know."

Therapist: "Take a taste of it and see what they are eating."

Sarah: "Greens"

Therapist: "Ask someone to call you by your name and see what name comes to you."

Sarah: "Maddie"

Therapist: "Good, look around. It is probably dark there except for the fire. Look around and see who the other people are."

Sarah: "I know their my family."

Therapist: "Look at Maddie and tell me about how old is she?"

Sarah: "Forty or fifty."

Therapist: "Does she have a husband there?"

Sarah: "I don't think so."

Therapist: "Does she have children there with her?"

Sarah: "Yes"

Therapist: "Look around and tell me how many children she has."

Sarah: "Four"

Therapist: "How does she feel about her children."

Sarah: "She loves them."

Therapist: "How do they treat Maddie, are they good to her?"

Sarah: "They don't work hard enough."

Therapist: "I'm going to take you to the next main event in Maddie's life counting there three, two, one, plant your feet firmly there, is Maddie indoors or out?"

Sarah: "She's outdoors. She's with a horse. She's leading the horse."

Therapist: "As she is leading the horse what happens next?"

Sarah: "Nothing."

Therapist: "I'm going to count you to the time when Maddie got married or got pregnant, counting you back to the first time Maddie was with a man, three, two, one, was Maddie indoors or out?"

Sarah: "Indoors"

Therapist: "Describe the indoors."

Sarah: "It's a shack similar to hers. It has a place where you cook and a bed. Very simple."

Therapist: "Is she alone or is someone with her?"

Sarah: "She's alone."

Therapist: "What happens next?"

Sarah: "She's gonna get whipped." CLIENTS SPEECH AND ACCENT HAS CHANGED

Therapist: "Who is going to whip her?"

Sarah: "Her master."

Therapist: "What is causing her to get whipped?"

Sarah: "She did something. She is afraid she is gonna get whipped. She's hiding out."

Therapist: "How does she feel?"

Sarah: "Afraid."

Therapist: "Tell me what happens next?"

CLIENT DOES NOT ANSWER WHICH SIGNALS A TRAMA AND REPRESSED MEMORY. I SUSPECT MADDIE GOT WHIPPED BY HER MASTER.

Therapist: "Go to the first time Maddie becomes pregnant."

Sarah: "She's with a boy. A boy who lives there too."

Therapist: "How does she feel about the boy?"

Sarah: "She likes him, but they have to sneak."

Therapist: "How does he feel about her?"

Sarah: "He likes her too."

Therapist: "How does Maddie feel when she gets pregnant?"

Sarah: "Happy, but scared."

Therapist: "How does the boy feel?"

Sarah: "The same way."

Therapist: "Does Maddie know where she lives?"

Sarah: "I don't know."

Therapist: "It's Ok, a lot of times when you don't know how to read or write, it's hard to know where you live. I'm going to take Maddie to the next main event in her life. Three, two, one, go to the next main event. Is she indoors or outdoors?"

Sarah: "Indoors, she's having a baby."

Therapist: "What's happening?"

Sarah: "It's hard even though this is not her first baby, it's hard."

Therapist: "Is she having difficulty?"

Sarah: "Yes, there are other women there, but it's hard. She is in a lot of pain."

Therapist: "Is she scared too?"

Sarah: "Uh huh."

Therapist: "Where is she feeling that feeling?"

Sarah: "All over her body."

Therapist: "Have her be there with her baby. What happens, does she finally give birth?"

Sarah: "Yes, the baby's fine."

Therapist: "How is Maddie doing?"

Sarah: "She's fine, she's tough."

Therapist: "Does she still have to sneak to see her boyfriend?"

Sarah: "No, I feel like he's around."

Therapist: "How does Maddie feel about having another baby?"

Sarah: "She's glad it's over. She's happy."

Therapist: "I'm going to take you to the next main event, counting to the next main event, one, two, three."

Sarah: "She's getting married."

Therapist: "How is she feeling?"

Sarah: "She's happy."

Therapist: "Be there with the wedding, are there others there? Is her family there?"

Sarah: "She doesn't have that much family. I don't know if she is not with them, but everyone there is supportive of her."

Therapist: "I am guessing having a family is very important to Maddie."

Sarah: "It is."

Therapist: "I am going to take you to the next main event in Maddie's life – is she indoors or out?"

Sarah: "Outdoors."

Therapist: "Describe the outdoors."

Sarah: "It's like a field."

Therapist: "What is she doing out there in the field?"

Sarah: "She's working hard, she's tired."

Therapist: "I'm going to take you to the next main event in Maddie's life, three, two, one, plant your feet firmly there."

Sarah: "She's laying down now."

Therapist: "Is her husband there?"

Sarah: "No, he's gone."

Therapist: "I'm going to take you to the time right before the husband left, are they indoors or out?"

Sarah: "Outside."

Sarah: "He dropped down. He was outside working; he dropped down, something happened to him. She's upset, she's screaming and crying. He dropped down; I don't know what was wrong with him."

Therapist: "Now Maddie is left alone with the children."

Sarah: "They are older now."

Therapist: "I am going to take you to a time when Maddie was having conflict with her husband, counting one, two, three, are they indoors or out?"

Sarah: Indoors. "He wants to leave. He wants to take the family and leave the place. He wants to go to another place, but she doesn't want to. She tells him to stop talking like that."

Therapist: "He wants to leave, but she doesn't want him to."

Sarah: "Where are they going to go?"

Therapist: "So they are free to leave now?"

Sarah: "No, why would he do that. Why would he even suggest that?"

Therapist: "So arguing with him is very scary for you?"

Sarah: "She's angry. He knows it's not safe for the kids; it's not safe for them. Where are they going to go? They would be found."

Therapist: "Do they argue much about this?"

Sarah: "No."

Therapist: "So when your brother is arguing with your mother – where does the fear come from?"

Sarah: "I don't know. I don't like arguing, I like things to go smoothly."

Therapist: "With Maddie, did things go pretty smooth?"

Sarah: "Yes, because she demanded it. She demanded things go smoothly and he knew it."

Therapist: "Maddie was a strong loving woman, but afraid to take risks. I want you to go right there before Maddie dies, is she indoors or out?"

Sarah: "She's indoors; she's in the same shack. She is not feeling well. There are people with her. She knows she is dying, she just knows."

Therapist: "Stay there with her and let me know when she can look down on herself."

Sarah: "Now."

Therapist: "How is she feeling?"

Sarah: "Good."

Therapist: "I want you to have her look back on that lifetime and tell me what lessons could she have learned from that lifetime."

Sarah: "She was a good and loving person. Her family was very important to her."

Therapist: "What about freedom for her, was that important."

Sarah: "Not as important as having her family safe and taking care of her family."

Therapist: "I want you to imagine there is a beam of light coming down." THERAPIST WENT ON TO THE INTEGRATION AND HEALING PART OF THE SESSION. CLIENT WAS THEN BROUGHT OUT OF THE HYPNOTIC STATE.

Sarah talked about how vivid the life of Maddie felt to her and then revealed that she and her husband had been fighting a lot lately. He had been laid off from his job and decided this was a good time to open his own business. Sarah was afraid as it threatened the family's financial security since she was now the bread winner and wanted her husband to get a safe secure job. She understood how Maddie's fear was impacting her own life and inability to support her husband's dreams. Realizing this was not a life threatening situation and that one of her Karmic lessons was to learn how to take a risk, Sarah felt ready to support her husband with his business plans.

As one can also expect, Sarah is a wonderful caring mother who like Maddie, really loves her family and they are the most important part of her life. At my request, Sarah wrote about the experience of going through Past Life Regression.

"I have to admit that while I was very excited about having the regression done, I was very skeptical that it was real. Once we started, I had quite a bit of anxiety about what was going to happen. During the experience, I tried to be open-minded and relax, but it was very difficult at first. I did not expect to get as emotional as I did, and I especially didn't expect to cry! I could tell that you were trying to get me to go beyond this current lifetime, but for some reason my mind was very resistant. It was hard to tell if what I was seeing was real or imagined, so I didn't trust it. I am normally a very grounded and concrete person, so I had to try hard to let my mind go. It got much easier after a while, and at one point I actually felt all the emotions that Maddie was experiencing while seeing her husband lying dead on the ground.

The image of Maddie the slave has stuck with me ever since the regression. I am honestly still a little skeptical as to whether or not I imaged her, but the discussion we had afterwards made me appreciate that it didn't matter either way. The longer I have sat and thought about the experience, the more revelations I have about it. Somehow, Maddie seems to be a part of me. Even as I write this, I just realized that I have always felt connected to slaves. Now I understand why. Yes, they are a part of my heritage as a Black woman, but I have always felt that I knew what they went through.

I am very thankful for the experience. I learned a great deal about myself. Maddie and I are very much alike, particularly in how we view the world. I am now significantly more aware of when I am not allowing myself to take risks. I am having a very hard time dealing with this trait, but I plan to keep working on it. Knowing something intellectually is one thing, but experiencing it with such a deep emotional and spiritual connection is unlike anything I can describe. Maddie taught me a good lesson about how I can improve my life. I realize that I am holding back from doing a lot of things out of fear. I'm having an emotional reaction even writing this. In the future, I would love to do more regressions. But, I know that this time I saw exactly what I needed to see. Thank you."

Paul's Regression

O ne of the most significant research subjects that I was lucky enough to work with was Paul (name changed for confidentiality). Paul was an exterminator and actually came to my home to get rid of some rats in my attic. The metaphor was certainly appropriate at the time as I had just moved from Santa Fe, New Mexico and found Florida to be really shocking as it was filled with human rats and much distress as some of my neighbors were very unkind to one another, I kept paying people to do work for me. The therapist supervisor where I worked at a detox center treated clients and staff with unbearable disrespect. Someone was trying to rip me off on a regular basis and I found the culture in Orlando to be much different than what I experienced in Santa Fe. I was plagued with regret and doubt about leaving New Mexico.

Paul seemed to be the first really intelligent, well read, and genuinely nice person I had met in Orlando. This is not to say that there are not plenty of intelligent and nice people in Orlando, I just had not met them, except for Paul. He could talk about history, science, philosophy and politics. His career choice and his intelligence level did not match and so I thought he would be an interesting subject for me to regress.

Paul reported that "he had feelings of success and yet could not attain what he perceived to be success". He claimed that he was an agnostic and did not believe in reincarnation, but he was a willing subject although he was not sure that he could be hypnotized.

Paul was born December 31, 1946 in Nicaragua. He came to the United States in December of 1981 and was married two years later to his current wife. The couple enjoys a good marriage and they shared the birth of one son and two daughters. While living in Nicaragua, Paul attended college for economics and worked in the field. In April 1978, Paul joined the resistance and was a Sandinista Rebel from April 1978 until July 1979. While acting as part of the Nicaraguan resistance, Paul killed the enemy and mutilated bodies during battles. He also suffered from Post-Traumatic Stress Disorder caused by the war and the horrors of battle. While Paul was interested in addressing issues dealing with his PTSD, he was also interested in finding out what held him back from succeeding in the corporate environment.

Paul reported after his regression that, "he has been a seeker of truth and the regressions opened doors of understanding for him". He also reported that the regressions "helped me to be more at peace with myself and that the process of regression has helped me greatly".

What is most important about Paul is that he was able to give information and details about his past life that we were able to investigate and verify. Further validation came from an assistant Professor of History at Lebanon Valley College named Michael Schroeder who very generously shared information from his website and thesis. I had just happened to come across his website late one evening accidently. To add to the synchronicity, I grew up in Lebanon, Pennsylvania which is where Professor Schroeder had just moved. It seems somehow the universe has a way of bringing collectives of information full circle something like the five degrees of separation.

The same hypnotic inductions were done with Paul as were done with my other subjects. The process took approximately thirty minutes since the client had some resistance to the process.

Transcript

Therapist: "How are you feeling?"

Paul: "I feel lost and heavy."

Therapist: "Where in your body do you most feel the feelings of being lost and heavy. Check in with your body, where do you feel lost and heavy."

Paul: "My legs are heavy, my lips are heavy."

Therapist: "Feel the heaviness in your lips – if it were a color what color would that heaviness be?"

Paul: "Black"

Therapist: "Go into the black color, feel the energy – feel the emptiness, being heavy, not being able to speak the words – speak your truth. Counting you back to the first time you felt that same heavy feelings in your lips. One, two, three, go right there to the first time you felt that same have feeling in your lips."

Paul: "Black"

Therapist: "Go into the black energy, into the heaviness; go into the energy that holds you back. Fee the energy now (loud clap of hands) release the energy. Close your eyes. How do you feel now?"

Paul: "Numb – I feel numb in my face, numb in my hands, numb in my lips."

Therapist: "Go into that numbness in your face, hands, and lips."

Paul: "Very numb, very numb."

Tristan: "Go into that numb feeling. What color would that numb feeling be?"

Paul: "No color."

Therapist: "I want you to release all that energy, all that dark energy that has held you back from being the person that you wanted to be. I want you to find your potential and release all the energy like a dark cloud around your face, hands, and lips. Bring that dark energy and dark cloud out that holds you away from source. (Loud Clap) Release the energy, release the heaviness, release the darkness, release the dark energy that has been holding you for so long, that has held you from realizing your potential. Release all the dark energy. Tell me how you fell pulling the numbness up, releasing all the darkness, releasing all the dark energy that has held you for so long from speaking your truth."

Paul: "My knees are less numb; my nose is numb."

Therapist: "Let's go into that and release all the numbness, imagine dark clouds moving from your head, your nose, and your eyes. We are going to bring those dark clouds of energy out from your head. All that negative energy is going to leave so it cannot have any more power over you. Release all the dark energy. It is moving out of the room through the sky. Move down through your chest, abdomen, legs, feet, pushing the dark clouds of energy out releasing all the tension releasing all the negative dark energy. I am going to count one, two, three, releasing the energy pulling it to the surface." (Loud clap)

"Your whole body is starting to feel lighter and now imagine a white beam of light coming down into the top of your head and it is going to push out all of the dark energy that has held you back. Feeling your face, head, lips, the light is healing you, restoring you, you can feel the light travel down through your body. The light is healing you, the light is taking away the pain, it is taking away the heaviness. You will be able to find the causes, find the things that have stopped you from being successful moving deeper and deeper down. I want you to start counting from fifty backwards and the numbers will begin to fade away and then a TV screen will appear."

Paul: "50, 49, 48, 47, and so on.........client counts down to one backwards."

Therapist: "Now see a large TV screen. On the screen are images from your past a scene from your past."

Paul: "Light, purple and green."

Therapist: "Look into the purple and as you look at the purple have it form a TV screen. Imagine a scene from the past - A scene with your family, your parents, a scene from the past."

Paul: "I am seeing myself in a chair. I am holding my son on my chest. I am wearing a white tee shirt."

Therapist: "How are you feeling there holding your son?"

Paul: "I am feeling a tenderness."

Therapist: "Where are you feeling that love and tenderness?"

Paul: "In my chest."

Therapist: "What would that energy say if it could speak?"

Paul: "I love him."

Therapist: "Feel the energy of the little infant lying there on your chest – so safe, feel his energy. If that infant's energy could speak what would it say?"

Paul: "Safe."

Therapist: "Now go into that energy of being loving, what color would that energy be if it were a color."

Paul: "Baby blue."

Therapist: "Go into that warm loving feeling in your chest. I am going to count you back to the first time and place you remember feeling that same warm feeling in your chest. One, two, three, are you indoors or outdoors?"

Paul: "Outdoors."

Therapist: "Describe the outdoors."

Paul: "Green with palms."

Therapist: "What are you wearing on your feet?"

Paul: "I am on my father's chest. He is swimming. I am on top of him. I am about three or four."

Therapist: "Be there with your father. How does that feel?"

Paul: "Safe."

Therapist: "Feel your father's energy. How is your father feeing?"

Paul: "He loves me."

Therapist: "How else does he feel about his son?"

Paul: "He is worrying." (unable to understand what client is saying)

Therapist: "Are you happy?"

Paul: "Yes."

Therapist: "Where do you feel that energy the most of being with your father?"

Paul: "In my chest, very relaxed."

Therapist: "Go back into that good feeling, loving feeling in your chest – feel that energy. Enjoy you experience with your father. Now go back to the very first time you felt that same feeling. Plant your feet firmly, where are you, indoors or out?"

Paul: "I am out."

Therapist: "Describe the outdoors."

Paul: "I am with fruit trees."

Therapist: "What trees?"

Paul: "Mangoes. I am with my mother. My mother is taking care of me."

Therapist: "What's happening there?"

Paul: "I just fell. I am hurt."

Therapist: "Look at your face, tell me how old you are?"

Paul: "Two."

Therapist: "What kind of baby are you? I think you are adventuresome."

Paul: "I am bleeding from my Lip. My mother is taking care of me. She cleaned my lip."

Therapist: "How does that feel having your mother taking care of you?"

Paul: "She is young! She is very slim."

Therapist: "Notice everything about your mother."

Paul: "She looks very nice."

Therapist: "Can you smell her skin?"

Paul: "Yes."

Therapist: "Go into her energy there. How is she feeling there as she is holding you in her arms?"

Paul: "She is happy. There is the house where I was born."

Therapist: "Have your mother take you to the house, go into the house. Is there anyone else in the house?"

Paul. "Grandma, Papa Reina, dog with blue eye."

Therapist: "How does the family feel about each other? Are your mother and father happy?"

Paul: "They respect each other; they respect the grandparents."

Therapist: "They respect the grandparents, but what caused them to be together? Go into your mother's energy when she is in the house."

Paul: "She takes me out we walk, she sits with me, she loves me, she holds me, she feeds me, she makes me feel secure."

Therapist: "Where are you feeling that love in your body?"
Paul: "Sweet."

Therapist: "Where do you feel those feelings in your body, the love, the nurturing, where do you feel that energy?"

Paul: "All over my body."

Therapist: "Go into that energy, that wonderful nurturing energy, feel that all through the body."

Paul: "Is this a dream or is this really happening."

Therapist: "Yes, it is really happening. I am going to count you back to the first time you felt that same sense of being loved and nurtured. Plant your feet firmly there, are you indoors or outdoors?"

Paul: "I cannot say, I cannot tell."

Therapist: "Tell me what is happening now."

Paul: "I am standing by some kind of canvas."

Therapist: "Look at your feet, what are you wearing on your feet?"

Paul: …..(no reply)

Therapist: "Tell me are you inside or out?"

Paul: "I don't know. I am an adult."

Therapist: "Look at your hair, is it long or short."

Paul: "I have big hair, long hair."

Therapist: "Tell me if you are young or old?"

Paul: "Young adult."

Therapist: "Tell me what you are wearing?"

Paul: "Very wide pants, very wide sleeves, print shirt, open chest."

Therapist: "Are you alone or are there others with you?"

Paul:…(no reply)

Therapist: "Describe where you are."

Paul: "It's like a canvas tent."

Therapist: "What happens next? Look at the furniture."

Paul: "It is pretty rustic; there is a table and hurricane lamp."

Therapist: "Tell me what happens next while you are there in the tent."

Paul: "The image is gone."

Therapist: "Go back there, back to the image. You are in the tent, now go outside of the tent. Go outside and describe what you see."

Paul: "There is a forest."

Therapist: "Look around and describe the forest."

Paul: "Mountains, I am at the edge of the forest where grass has started growing down the hills."

Therapist: "What kind of a day is it?"

Paul: "Sunny."

Therapist: "Tell me what happens next."

Paul: "Nothing."

Therapist: "Go right back there, follow the energy back, you are there at the edge of the forest, look around."

Paul: "Yeah, I can see...."(client describes scene in Spanish and English, but I am unable to understand what he is saying on the tape.)

Paul: "There is a ravine."

Therapist: "How are you feeling?"

Paul: "I don't know what I am doing there. I have no purpose."

Therapist: "I want you to go to a mealtime, a place where that person has their meals – is he indoors or out?"

Paul: "I am in the tent. I am alone."

Therapist: "Listen for his name, what is his name?"

Paul: "He does not want to be found, he does not want anyone to know his name."

Therapist: "I am going to take him to the time and place that caused him to go to the forest, counting back one, two, three. Is he indoors or outdoors?"

Paul: "I cannot see."

Therapist: "I am going to take you to the next main event in his life, counting one, two, three."

Paul: "He is in the canvas tent. He is hiding."

Therapist: "I want you to have him speak his name. Listen for his name; listen for him to say his name."

Paul: "Pedron"

Therapist: "Be there with Pedron. Have him have a meal. What does he eat for his meal?"

Paul: "Sundried meat."

Therapist: "How does Pedron feel at mealtime?"

Paul: "He is hungry, he is big and muscular."

Therapist: "Look at his face, listen for his name."

Paul: "Pedro Altamirano"

Client immediately comes out of hypnosis sitting straight up after saying the name. He looks a bit dazed and confused. The client states he does not understand. He knows who Pedron Altamirano is as he is a famous military leader of the Sandinistas from the turn of the century. He was especially known for his grizzly acts of war cutting off the heads of his victims and gutting them. My client is visibly shaken and clearly wants to disengage from his experience as he does not want to think of himself as this ruthless killer.

Since the energy and cellular memory from the past has just been tapped into and not transmuted through conscious understanding it is important for the client to undergo another regression in a week after he has digested the experience. Paul returns a week later for his second session to find out what holds him back in his life and to heal himself from depression.

Paul's Second Regression

Therapist: "Use your torch light to help you see the boxes. Let me know when you find your box by saying now out loud. I want you to describe your box to me."

Paul: "Wood, painted."

Therapist: "Tell me what is painted on the box."

Paul: "Little circles."

Therapist: "What color is the box?"

Paul: "White, red, blue, with some green circles."

Therapist: "How big is the box?"

Paul: "About one foot each side."

Therapist: "Now I want you to use your torch light and open the box. Tell me what you see inside the box."

Paul: "Nothing."

Therapist: "I want you to look inside the nothing. What does the inside of the box look like?"

Paul: "There is a light in the room."

Therapist: "How does that light make you feel?"

Paul: "It erased everything."

Therapist: "Stay with the light, it is here to help you and guide you. Tell me what is the light doing now?"

Paul: INAUDIBLE

Therapist: "Tell me what the light is doing."

Paul: "It's erased everything."

Therapist: "Tell the light you need to understand. Ask the light to let you see the past. Ask the light to show you a symbol. Tell the light you need to have understanding. What symbol does the light show you?"

Paul: "Chains, everything blanc, (Spanish word) I'm in the clouds."

Therapist: "You're in the clouds, how do you feel in the clouds?"

Paul: "I'm floating."

Therapist: "How do you feel floating there in the clouds?"

Paul: "Weightless." THIS IS A SIGN OF RESISTANCE AS THE PSYCHE IS TRYING TO ESCAPE THE MEMORIES BY DETOURING TO A MORE ESOTERIC SPACE.

Therapist: "Enjoy that feeling of floating. I'm going to count you back there to that lifetime of Pedro. I am going to count you back to his boyhood when he is having a mealtime with his family. Three, two, one, go right back there to that time and place when Pedro is having a mealtime with his family. Is he indoors or outdoors?"

Paul: "He's outdoors right outside his house. The house is wood and tin roof. There are many ivy vines outside the house."

Therapist: "How does he feel as a young boy outside his house?"

Paul: "He's eating strips of meat."

Therapist: "What else is happening, is he with his family?"

Paul: "Yes."

Therapist: "Who are they?"

Paul: "There is somebody else."

Therapist: "Have Pedro look at his feet. What is he wearing on his feet?"

Paul: "Back shoes."

Therapist: "Look at his clothing. What clothing is he wearing?"

Paul: "White pants." THE REST IS INAUDIBLE

Therapist: "Look at his hands, are they big or small?"

Paul: "Big for a boy."

Therapist: "Look at his hair is it long or short."

Paul: "He is wearing a hat?"

Therapist: "Look at his face about how old is Pedro."

Paul: "Five, six or seven."

Therapist: "How does he feel there?"

Paul: "He is a happy boy."

Therapist: "Where does he feel that feeling of happiness the most?"

Paul: INAUDIBLE, EXCEPT SOMETHING ABOUT THE WOMEN

Therapist: "Tell me about the women, how does Pedro feel about the women?"

Paul: Mom and aunt."

Therapist: "Is there anyone else there?"

Paul: "Father, he is smoking a wooden pipe."

Therapist: "How does Pedro feel about his father?"

Paul: "He protects him."

Therapist: "How does Pedro feel about his mother?"

Paul: "He cares. She cares."

Therapist: "How does Pedro feel about his family?"

Paul: "It was a lot of responsibilities."

Therapist: "Does Pedro go to school?"

Paul: "Yes, he walks down the hill."

Therapist: "Does he live in a village or the country?"

Paul: "There is no village only country."

Therapist: "Where does he live?"

Paul: "El Vilgaro….There is sugar cane, I can see Elcapiche. They came and smashed the sugar cane." (spelling can be off on many of the Spanish names.)

Therapist: "Who came and smashed the sugar cane."

Paul: "Two big cylinders." DIALOG BECOMES INAUDIBLE

Therapist: "Is Pedro watching as they harvest the sugar cane?"

Paul: "Yes, I saw them cutting, carrying the sugar cane to Elcapiche."

Therapist: "I am going to take you to the next main event in Pedro's life. Counting one, two, three, going to the next main event, is he indoors or outdoors?"

Paul: "He's outdoors. He is in the city."

Therapist: "Look at his face, about how old is he now?"

Paul: "He is a young man."

Therapist: "How is he feeling there in the city?"

Paul: "He feels very important."

Therapist: "What makes him feel very important?"

Paul: "He is wearing a suit."

Therapist: "Where did he get the suit?"

Paul: "It came in the luggage."

Therapist: "Where did he get the luggage?"

Paul: "It came from the train."

Therapist: "Did Pedro take the luggage?"

Paul: "Three more men, I am loading the luggage."

Therapist: "Look at the men, how does Pedro know these men?"

Paul: "They came for a meeting."

Therapist: "I am going to take you to the meeting. Be right there at the meeting and tell me what is happening?"

Paul: "There is a lot of people, everybody's wearing suits. There is Agusto!"

Therapist: "Who is Augusto?"

Paul: "My friend, he looks so little."

Therapist: "Was he from the country where you lived?"

Paul: "Yes, he is our leader."

Therapist: "Tell me his name."

Paul: "Augusto Sandino"

Therapist: "Is he older than you?"

Paul: "Three or four years."

Therapist: "Tell me how do you feel about Augusto?"

Paul: "I can die for him."

Therapist: "Tell me what they are discussing there at the meeting."

Paul: "He is the center of the meeting."

Therapist: "What are they discussing there?"

Paul: INAUDIBLE

Therapist: "Do you know where this person is from?"

Paul: "He is from the United States."

Therapist: "What is he there for?"

Paul: "We are meeting in Mexico City. There will be many people there."

Therapist: "What are you doing in Mexico City? What brings everyone together there?"

Paul: "He is starting to talk."

Therapist: "What does he say?"

Paul. "Welcome brothers. Another person is starting to talk. He is from Spain. His accent is from Madrid."

Therapist: "People are coming from all over. What are they coming together for?"

Paul: "For our organization."

Therapist: "What is your organization?"

Paul: CLIENT GIVES NAME IN SPANISH

Therapist: "What does that mean?"

Paul: "The World Brotherhood"

Therapist: "What are they discussing at the meeting?"

Paul: "Bringing goodness to the world."

Therapist: "How do they propose to bring goodness to the world?"

Paul: "We'll work and have communities, increase the numbers of the brotherhood."

Therapist: "How is Pedro feeling there at this meeting?"

Paul: "I was waiting a long time to be here."

Therapist: "Pedro has good intentions; he is a strong and good man. I am going to take you to the next main event in Pedron's life. I am going to count you there three, two, one, go right there to the next main event. Is he indoors or outdoors?"

Paul: "We are in the field."

Therapist: "What is happening in the field?"

Paul: "We are worried."

Therapist: "What are you worried about?"

Paul: "The government. The government doesn't want our soulness."

Therapist: "What is that?"

Paul: "The Masons."

Therapist: "What are they doing to the Masons?"

Paul: "They are putting them in Jail."

Therapist: "Are the Masons the same as the World Brotherhood?"

Paul: "Yes."

Therapist: "How does Pedron feel about the government?"

Paul: "Angry."

Therapist: "I am going to take you to the next main event in Pedron's life. Counting you there three, two, one, are you indoors or outdoors?"

Paul: "We are riding horses. We are going to fight."

Therapist: "Who are you going to fight?"

Paul: "The government forces and Yankies."

Therapist: "And who are Yankies?"

Paul: "American soldiers."

Therapist: "I want you to go there to the midst of the battle. How do you feel there fighting the government and American soldiers?"

Paul: "We must get rid of the Yankies."

Therapist: "How do you feel there in battle? Do you feel scared, powerful, how does it make you feel?"

Paul: "I don't have feelings. Carlos is with me. Carlos Hernendez."

Therapist: "Tell me what rank are you now?"

Paul: "I don't have rank."

Therapist: "Are you in charge?"

Paul: "Yes, they call me general."

Therapist: "How do you feel about the cause?"

Paul: "They lie, there is lying, putting papers throughout the communities. They say we want them to become communists. We are not communists."

Therapist: "You have an idea of doing what in your country?"

Paul: "We want to free this land from the oppressor. After we free the land there will be peace and everyone will be better."

Therapist: "Yes, so you have good ideas for your country. Where do you feel those feelings in your body?"

Paul: "Someone is coming. We stop the horses."

Therapist: "What happens next?"

Paul: "Two guys are coming to report."

Therapist: "What do they report?"

Paul: "They say there are some troops from the government. They say we are outnumbered."

Therapist: "What do you do next?"

Paul: "We will fight in a very wooded area. I call the commanders."

Therapist: "And then what do you do?"

Paul: "We will divide into four groups."

Therapist: "And will you fight?"

Paul: "Yes."

Therapist: "And now we are going to count you back to right after the battle. Three, two, one, do you win or lose?"

Paul: "We have not started. They approach on foot."

Therapist: "And then what happens?"

Paul: "They went to get rid of the guards and then they charge over the hill."

Therapist: "What do you do next?"

Paul: "I'm waiting. Two pistols. Say now! Start shooting! Start shooting!"

Therapist: "What happens next?"

Paul: "They used swords, we had pistols with long blades. The army was surprised."

Therapist: "Did you win the battle?"

Paul: "We killed everyone."

Therapist: "What did you do after that?"

Paul: "My men started to dismember them."

Therapist: "What reason did you do that?"

Paul: "We wanted the rest of the troops to see what would happen."

Therapist: "So you did it as a scare tactic."

Paul: "Yes, we hung the Yankees and we dismembered the rest of the troops."

Therapist: "And who's decision is that?"

Paul: "We have to stop them."

Therapist: "So you are very serious about winning and freeing the people."

Paul: "We must free them from the tyrant. He called the Americans."

Therapist: "What are some of the things he did to the people?"

Paul: "They closed the universities. All the intellectuals were jailed. They bring the American forces because they have friends in the American government."

Therapist: "What did the American government care about what was happening there?"

Paul: "The mines. They wanted the gold of the country. Lalionessa, Ceiona, Sundramonk." (I am not sure about the spelling of these mines.)

Therapist : "What other things did the Americans want there."

Paul: "They are cutting the forest."

Therapist: "How did the people feel as their forests are being cut and what was happening in the country?"

Paul: "They did not understand. Most of the people are illiterate. The University students were trying to educate the people. The gold and the forest belong to us. The telegraph is American property. They say the communist want to take over, but that is not true."

Therapist: "I am going to count Pedron to a Mason meeting during the time of the struggle. Three, two, one, plant your feet firmly there and tell me what is happening. Are there many people?"

Paul: "Yes."

Therapist: "Tell me what is happening."

Paul: INAUDIBLE…. "There is a Frenchman at the meeting and he has a woman translator."

Therapist: "What causes him to be there?"

Paul: "He is going to take our cause to Europe."

Therapist: "What do you want to happen?"

Paul: "Europeans will pressure the United States to take out their troops so we can finish our rebellion. Dr. Jose Estrada is there; he is a Dr. of philosophy. He is not teaching anymore. We are trying to protect him."

Therapist: "How do you come to try to protect him?"

Paul: "He is the head of the Mason Brotherhood."

Therapist: "He is very important. Is the government after him?"

Paul: "Yes."

Therapist: "I am going to count you to the next main event in Pedron's life. Plant your feet firmly there, three, two, one, are you indoors or outdoors?"

Paul: "Indoors. Wood floor, wood ceiling, white walls."

Therapist: "Are you alone or are there others with you?"

Paul: "My wife. She is sick, very sick."

Therapist: "What is wrong with her?"

Paul: "She has an ugly sickness. She has tuberculosis."

Therapist: "How does he feel about her?"

Paul: "Sorry, guilty."

Therapist: "Where are you feeling that guiltiness in your body?"

Paul: "I left her too long."

Therapist: "Where do you feel that guiltiness?"

Paul. "In my chest. I have someone else. Teresa."

Therapist: "Do you love her?"

Paul: "I love her. I love my wife."

Therapist: "Go into that guilty feeling in your chest and if that guilt could speak what would that guilt say?"

Paul: "She's going to die, I can't save her."

Therapist: "What do you do, do you stay with her or do you leave?"

Paul: "I stay with her, but she pushes me away. She is afraid I will be sick, but I kiss her anyway. I don't care."

Therapist: "How do you feel with the revolution and your wife's sickness?"

Paul: "I am worried about Augusto. He was invited by the president. I am worried they will double-cross him."

Therapist: "Tell me what happens. Do they double-cross him?"

Paul: "Yes, I begged him not to go. I cried in front of my men. My men see me crying, but I don't care."

Therapist: "He would not listen."

Paul: "He thought it was a chance for peace, but I knew he would be killed."

Therapist: "Where do you feel that helplessness? Where do you feel that wanting to stop him in your body now?"

Paul: "Maria died."

Therapist: "Are you having a hard time feeling things now?"

Paul: "I am confused. I want to spend some days in solitary. I take Teresa with me. We go to the place where I was happy."

Therapist: "Where did you go."

Paul: "To a hideout up in the mountains."

Therapist: "What happened there?"

Paul: "I see myself in a Déjà Vu. I have seen myself like this."

Therapist: "What happens next?"

Paul: "I see myself leaning against a post on the tent. Maria is dead. Teresa is bathing under a waterfall. I decide to go back."

Therapist: "Go back where?"

Paul: "I go back to my men. We go back to hide. We get news."

Therapist: "What happens next?"

Paul: "My thoughts were true. Augusto, his brother and three generals are killed."

Therapist: "How do you feel when you get the information?"

Paul: "Discouraged, desperate, angry."

Therapist: "What happens next?"

Paul: "The whole army is coming after me. Some traitors told them where we are located. Planes, shooting, bombs. Trucks filled with soldiers. They are everywhere."

Therapist: "What happens next?"

Paul: "I tell them to advance, but I know it is suicide. We advance from the front. My men say yes, but they know we will die. Some confess with the priest. They didn't want to go to hell, but I tell them hell is here. It is time to go. We run. I was hit."

Therapist: "Where were you hit?"

Paul: "Under my belt. I don't feel pain. I fall. I tell my men to shoot me. I don't want them to take me alive."

Therapist: "Does one of your men shoot you."

Paul: "No."

Therapist: "They love you so much."

Paul: "Yes. The soldiers hit me in the chest."

Therapist: "Tell me when you can look down on the battlefield."

Paul: "They found me. They are taking me."

Therapist: "Tell me what happens next."

Paul: "There is an American soldier. He is asking if that is me and they say yes."

Therapist: "And then what happens?"

Paul: "He comes with a sword and I tell him he is about to kill a real man. He puts the blade to my throat, but I don't feel any pain."

Therapist: "Are you fully in your body?"

Paul: "No."

Therapist: "What does he do now? Does he cut off your head?"

Paul: "Yes."

Therapist: "Tell Pedron to look back over his lifetime and tell me what lessons you could learn from that lifetime."

Paul: "I would do it again the same. One regret, Maria."

Paul: "I loved her. Augusto took his wife with him always. Maria was very sick."

Therapist: "You could not take her with you. You did the best for her that you could do. I want you to forgive yourself for Maria and for Augusto as you could not have saved them. He made his decision. Our energy knows no time or place. We all change roles coming in and out of each other's lives to help each other and to learn from each other. I want you to imagine a white light…". THE REGRESSION COMPLETES WITH A TIME FOR HEALING THE ENERGY BLOCKS, THE GUILT, AND TRANSMUTING ANY NEGATIVE ENERGY OR RESIDUE FROM THAT LIFETIME. PART OF THE HEALING ALSO INCLUDES HAVING THE PERSON EMBRACE ALL THAT HE WAS WITH ALL OF HIS FLAWS, FORGIVING MISTAKEN IDEAS AND ACCEPTING ALL OF THE POSITIVE ATTRIBUTES THAT IMBODIED HIS PAST LIFE SO HE CAN

FULLY LOVE THE PERSON THAT HE IS IN THE PRESENT. HE WILL ALSO HAVE A BETTER UNDERSTAND HIS LIFE FROM A KARMIC PERSPECTIVE. ONCE WE UNDERSTAND KARMA OR OUR LIFE LESSONS, IT NO LONGER HAS ANY HOLD OVER US.

All of the information given by Paul pertaining to Pedron was verified to be accurate. A skeptic could say he looked up the information before coming for the regression; however, the information about the mistress named Teresa was not easily accessible in books or on the computer. I was unable to find Teresa mentioned anywhere, but was able to verify her existence through the professor in Pennsylvania who did his thesis on Pedron.

Past life regressions are like the stuff of dreams as they open a story that lives deep in the experiences of our psyche. What is the real world and what is the dream world? How can we ever know for sure as all creation came from the "Word", "thought" and the "dream". There is an intelligence in dreams and the stories of regression that come from deep in the psyche which is related to a universal field of archetypes and symbols. The images of our dreams or our regressions are linked to a certain authenticity of our archetypal journey which whether real or imagined gives us insight, awareness, warnings, or guidance.

It is the archetypal patterns that inform the realities of our individual stories and give a universal quality to that which is essential to our own personal journey. It is most important to find the meaning in the stories and about the stories and not worry about whether the stories are flights of fancy, because they are true within the psyche.

By the testimony of each subject in this thesis, we are told that the regression therapy has brought about positive change in their lives and helped release them from experiencing symptoms of trauma. Additionally, each subject reported finding more meaning and fulfillment in their lives after having the regression therapy.

Conclusion

The current world is a rapidly changing place as our environments are besieged by natural disasters, wars wage in the Middle East as people struggle to achieve the ability to pursue happiness from tyrannical dictators, and corporate greed is ripping through the very fabric of civilization.

Trauma is all around us and yet how do we free ourselves from its effects as we feel our lives spinning more out of control as prices rise, jobs are lost, children are left homeless, and communities become isolated deserts of bureaucracy, elitism, apathy and disconnectedness.

We are not without hope and we are not without power in the face of such oppression. One is now called to the re-empowerment of the soul's journey and the hero must come forth courageously. The hero is the one who seeks for truth and knowledge no matter what the cost with a focused gaze at finding the prize and freeing himself from the sojourned quest. "Who am I? Why am I here? Where am I going?", once again becomes the battle cry from the philosopher's alchemical grist. We are called to the mysteries and burned in the cosmic caves to rise once again as the phoenix newly formed with a new understanding of who we truly are.

The tyranny of trauma which has kept us separated from the truth is now to be unveiled and we must recognize ourselves as the ever evolving spiritual beings that strive towards the cosmic consciousness of Nirvana. We must rejoice in our ability to relentlessly be resilient on our spiritual journey and recognize Karma as the great teacher.

We have been given free will out of love from the creator so we may choose to travel the journey of the spiritual path. We are like grown children finely groomed sent out by their parents to learn how to live on their own. The parent's love does not diminish for their children, but they must relinquish control and let their children learn how to survive on their own in the world so they can grow to full maturity. Even when our children fall to the way side besieged by selfish desires and childish ways we do not give up our love for them, nor does creator give up on us. This is the lesson of loving detachment. We wait, we pray and we hope for the best. As Creator wanted us to be free to choose our spiritual nature and connection to the cosmic Christ – Buddha – or whatever term you want to use, Creator bequests for us the experiential journey that we choose as our path to knowledge. No matter what good or great advice I might give to a client it is always left in their hands to make the choice.

By knowing our true energetic spiritual nature, we can give up bitterness and fear living life in gratitude knowing we can stop the cycle of destruction through our positive thoughts and good deeds. Peace of mind comes through the knowledge that we are not victims, but hero's traveling on a sometimes very dangerous, but exciting quest. By using discernment and mindfulness we can become better equipped to stay away from the dangerous pitfalls that might delay us from our spiritual awakening.

Our happiness lies within us and our ability to understand that the true self that we are, lives like a well spring waiting to be tapped. We must become proactive in our lives choosing wisely and releasing things that negatively impact us. We must not be confused by twisted thinking and stay focused on what we intuitively know to be congruent in our hearts and mind. We must lovingly embrace the world knowing that it is a world of sorrows and joy. As we look into each individual's face we must know they are a part of me, they want the same things I want only in varying degrees. And we must know that within serving others we gain some of the greatest joys.

Knowing that it is our desires and selfishness that has brought us to the traumas we face helps us to endure. With our lessons learned, Karma has lost its sting. Those things that kept us up at night are now put to rest and we find peace. In the midst of terrible things, we can find our power through connection and meditation, learning to exist in the NOW, free of all the negative mind chatter created from the past.

It has taken me much work to see that all the things that happen are just stories that we have become attached to. I know a woman who tells me every time I see her how her terrible childhood affects her. Her childhood has been done and over for twenty years, but the cellular memory of the woman keeps her trapped in her patterns unable to release what was negative and move forward to building a healthy life for herself. There is still a Karmic lesson that her soul craves to learn in the repeating of the story.

We must be vigilant in our process towards consciousness. The world is set up for hardship and we must not be discouraged from the processes that make us strong, courageous, and empowered. When we understand our spiritual nature and the continuity of the spiritual journey we are forever set free from trauma as death is just a transformation into another reality and what we do in ignorance is just a lesson to be learned.

If a rich person devoid of feeling for people less fortunate and who exploits others for his/her own gain could see the karmic debt that he/she was incurring, I doubt that he/she would still be so willing to continue his/her selfish acts. I am sure they would not. I also doubt that family members would so freely inflict emotional wounds on one another if they knew they would have to continue to repeat the patterns of abuse until they found realization of their ignorance. I wonder if men would continue to objectify women if they knew the extreme damage they would bring onto their own psyche as most likely they would become females in the next life taunted by their past karma. Could women perpetuate their own feelings of unworthiness if they knew they came into the world to heal the wounded goddess who has been laid to waste by a patriarchal society? Would politicians conspire to line their own pockets at the expense of the societies they represent and the environment that supports their quality of life, if they knew they would one day face retribution for their selfish acts?

One cardinal universal principle is that underlying all spiritual healing is that everything ultimately is resolved into the energy of consciousness. The biological medical model can only apply to what is manifest in the world of matter and as it can certainly help heal the body much like a mechanic fixes a car, true healing occurs on the spiritual energetic levels of existence. Given the choice between Prozac and regression therapy to heal trauma, I feel certain that the odds are much higher that one will find relief and sustaining healing through the process of regression therapy.

The wizard character "Harry Potter" uses a spell called "stupefy" which brings visions to me of medical doctors handing out their magical elixirs of Prozac, Zoloft, and Seroquel putting a spell of dullness on their unwitting patients. The ego is constantly supported by the past, deducting its conclusions from what it has experienced. If we stretch our timeline out beyond this life into past lives, we will see the experiences that inspired our current conditions. Freeing ourselves from the blocked energy that occurred due to trauma and bringing understanding of our spiritual journey into our conscious understanding through the process of regression therapy helps us heal ourselves from the inside out. Regression therapy is the catalyst for releasing us from the fear of death and the cycle of repeated negative habits that hold us prisoners in our own minds. When we truly know that we are divine and immortal, life becomes a wonderful adventure and we are the empowered hero who has finally found their holy grail.

I would be remiss if I did not address the true nature of existence for our human species. As science has proven that all matter can be reduced to energy, we must understand that even the physicality of our existence is reduced to energetic principles. The ancients knew this and wrote about it in their scriptures. Even King Solomon wrote a book of spells dealing with energetic principles and elementals.

Scientists often relegate this information to being mythology, or devised from the imagination, but they are wrong. There are four levels of distinct frequencies or levels of consciousness from which individuals operate whether they are aware of it or not. They are known as the etheric plane, mental plane, emotional/astral plane and the physical plane. These planes are like energetic grids which operate much like a radio wave as they collect data for the individual and for the collective. The earth as we experience it is formed through collective thought patterns and an encoded blueprint for existence.

The etheric plane holds the blueprint of life as spirit moves into matter. This plane contains collective and individual memories from this life and from past lives. These memories comprise the origination of the developmental path we are to travel in the physical.

The mental plane is the grid of individual and collective thought which forms the thinking aspects of the individual and the collective society that will most fulfill their needs. The collective thought also determines the direction societies take in developing their identity such as seen in the renaissance or the industrial age.

The emotional or astral plane is where the collective and the individual feelings are experienced. This plane is fraught with desires and illusions. The emotional plane in many ways is the entrapment plane as the emotional body is often reactionary and deceptive.

Fortunately, love, courage, compassion, and kindness are also products of the emotional plane that bring quality as well as consciousness to the expansion of human life.

The most commonly addressed plane of existence is that of the physical plane. This plane is that of the outer world that we experience as the world of matter which supports our existence in the physical realm.

Each plane of consciousness is held together by an element. The etheric plane is the element of fire. In the etheric plane energy becomes consumed and transmuted into pure cosmic consciousness. The mental plane holds the essence of air which relates to our thought processes. The emotional/astral plane is the element of water which is the catalyst for the unconscious processes. The physical plane is the element of earth which is where we find the elemental properties for our physical being.

This information pertaining to frequencies is important to ascertain as it points to the level of healing that should be addressed when dealing with trauma or any other natural issue of existence.

Clearly if one has a cut on their body or a broken leg they are dealing with the physical plane and the chemistry of earth elements. A doctor or medicine man would be the best solution for a good recovery.

If someone broke their leg due to being attacked that would then involve the emotional plane and the mental plane as their emotions might create a trauma and what they thought about the situation would create a perception. The etheric plane would only be utilized if the person could detach from the situation with total understanding, and of course this would be the ultimate goal.

Until we are able to recognize the totality of our human experience, we will fall short of finding solutions to treating trauma in its deepest effects. The medical model deals with the physical plane and while it has made great strides in the treatments of chemical processes of the physical realm, it falls gravely short in its treatment of the spiritual nature of the individual.

Until we fully embrace the fact that we are energetic spiritual beings taking up residence in a physical shell in order to be experiential in this world of matter, we are going to continue to miss our mark as having the capacity to be a positive co-creative force filled with the potential and ability to create a most amazing world filled with abundance for all. And this I know is true.

Bibliography

Cerminara, Gina. Many Mansions. New York, Penguin Books, 1991

Hunt, Morton M. Mental Hospital. New York, Pyramid Publications, 1961

Grof, Stanislav, M.D.. The Holotropic Mind. New York, Harper Collins Publishers, 1993

Doidge, Norman, M.D.. The Brain That Changes Itself. New York, Penguin Group, 2007

Weiss, Brian L. M.D.. Many Lives, Many Masters. New York, Simon & Schuster, Inc. 1988

Semkiw, Walter, M.D. Return Of The Revolutionaries. Charlottesville, Va. Hampton Roads Publishing Company, Inc. 2003

Cranston, Silvia. Reincarnation. Pasadena, California, Theosophical University Press. 1993

Pert, Candace, M.D.. Molecules of Emotion, New York, Scribner. 2003

Gehlek, Rimpoche Nawang. Good Life, Good Death. New York, Riverhead Books. 2001

Starhawk. In Beauty May I Walk. Watford, United Kingdom, Exley Publications. 1997

Plato. Great Dialogues Of Plato. New York, Penguin Group. 1956

McGee, Sophie. Trust and Faith. Philadelphia, Pennsylvania, Xlibris Corporation. 2008

Easwaran, Eknath, Translation. The Bhagavad Gita. New York, New York, Vantage Books. 2000

Bailey, Alice. The Soul The Quality Of Life. New York, New York, Lucis Publishing. 1974

Lamsa, George. Translation. Holy bible. Philadelphia, Pennsylvania, A.J. Holman Company. 1957

Zukav, Gary. The Seat Of The Soul. New York, New York, Simon & Schuster. 1989

Van den Beukel, Anthony. The Physicists and God. North Andover, Massachusetts, Genesis Publishing Company. 1995

Moody, Raymond M.D.. Life After Life. New York, New York, Bantam Books. 1975

Jung, C.G. Memories, Dreams, Reflections. New York, New York, Vintage Books. 1989

Becker, Ernest. Escape From Evil. New York, New York, The Free Press. 1975

Newton, Issac. Newton's Philosophy Of Nature. New York, New York, Hafner Publishing. 1953

Douglass, William C. M.D.. Busted. Baltimore, Maryland, Healthier News. 2009

Leek, Sybil. Reincarnation The Second Chance. Briarcliff Manor, New York, Stein and Day. 1974

Stevenson, Ian, M.D.. India Cases Of The Reincarnation Type Volume I. Charlottesville, Virginia, University Press of Virginia. 1975

Pearce, Joseph C. The Crack In The Cosmic Egg. New York, New York. Julian Press. 1971

Tulku, Tarthang. Sacred Dimensions of Time and Space. Berkley, California. Dharma Publishing. 1997

St. John Of The Cross. Dark Night Of The Soul. New York, New York, Doubleday Publishing. 1959

Saraydarian, Torkom. Breakthrough to Higher Psychism. West Hills, California, T.S.G. Publishing Foundation. 1990

Mitchell, Stephen. Translation. The Book Of Job. New York, New York, Harper Collins. 1986

Cooper, Jack R. The Biochemical Basis of Neurpharmacology. New York, New York, Oxford University Press. 1970

Oyle, Irving, PhD. Time Space & The Mind. Berkley, California, Celestial Arts. 1976

Pearson, E. Norman. Space, Time, and Self. Wheaton, Illinois, The Theosophical Publishing House. 1967

Narby, Jeremy. The Cosmic Serpent. New York, New York, Putnam Publishing. 1999

Murphy, Joseph, PhD.. The Cosmic Power. New York, New York, MJF Books. 1968

Robinson, James, Editor. The Nag Hammadi Library. New York, New York, HarperCollins Publishers. 1978

Boyne, Gil. Transforming Therapy. Glendale, California, Westwood Publishing. 1985

Cayce, Edgar. Modern Prophet. Avenel, New Jersey, Gramercy Books. 1967

King, Martin Luther, PhD. Why We Can't Wait. New York, New York. Penguin Books. 1963

Weiss, Brian. M.D.. Through Time Into Healing. New York, New York. Fireside Publishing 1992

Ross, Benjamin, M.D. The Blacklist. Baltimore, Maryland. Healthier News. 2009

Erickson, Milton H. My Voice Will Go With You. New York, New York, Norton & Company. 1991

Heisenberg, Werner. The Physical Principles of the Quantum Theory. Chicago, Illinois, University of Chicago Press. 1930

Caruth, Cathy. Trauma. Baltimore, Maryland. The John Hopkins University Press. 1995

Hunt, Valerie. Infinite Mind. Malibu, California, Malibu Publishing o. 1995

Lucas, Winafred, PhD.. Regression Therapy A Handbook For Professionals Vol I. Crest Park, California, Deep Forest Press. 1993

Lucas, Winafred, PhD.. Regression therapy A Handbook For Professionals Vol.II. Crest Park, California, Deep Forest Press. 1993

Schwartz, Gary, PhD.. The Living Energy Universe. Charlottesville, Virginia, Hampton Roads Publishing Company, Inc. 1999

Restak, Richard, PhD.. Receptors. New York, New York, Bantam Books. 1994

Norman, Ernest. The Infinite Concept of Cosmic Creation. El Cajon, California, Unarius, Science of Life. 1956

Goswami, Amit, PhD. Physics Of The Soul. Charlottesville, Virginia. Hampton Roads Publishing. 2001

Printed in the United States
By Bookmasters